MANAGING THE SPECIAL LIBRARY

Strategies for Success within the Larger Organization

by
Herbert S. White

Knowledge Industry Publications, Inc.
White Plains, NY and London

Professional Librarian Series

Managing the Special Library:
Strategies for Success within the Larger Organization

Library of Congress Cataloging in Publication Data

White, Herbert S.
  Managing the special library.

  Bibliography: p.
  Includes index.
  1. Libraries, Special—Administration.   2. Information
services—Administration.   I. Title.
Z675.A2W45   1984   025.5'276   83-24390
  ISBN 0-86729-088-9
  ISBN 0-86729-087-0 (pbk.)

Printed in the United States of America

10   9   8   7   6   5   4   3   2   1

Table of Contents

To my wife, Virginia

Helpmate - Critic - Mentor

Preface

More than 30 years as a special librarian, association official and now library school teacher have not succeeded in quelling my sense of continuing surprise that the special library profession exists as a recognizable entity. After all, aerospace information specialists, art museum slide librarians, bank and brokerage firm information center managers, and government information center administrators would on the face of it appear to have very little in common. The fact that obviously they think they do—and have acted on that premise by organizing into vigorous and rapidly expanding professional associations—is a clear indication that they appear to know who and what they are. By extension, they also know who and what they are not.

When in 1975 I first taught a course in special librarianship, I faced the task of isolating and spotlighting some of the characteristics shared by special libraries. A class of 30 students, some interested in physics and chemistry information, some in journalism and advertising, some in historical museums and archives, and many not sure, does not provide a simple common denominator. I have observed the same mixture as a teacher of continuing education seminars for special librarians.

Special librarians *do* have a unique quality, and I still do not know the extent to which the task molds the individual, or the degree to which the individual adapts the job to himself or herself. This book is part of that continuing exploration into what special library and information center managers are, and what makes them different.

It is within this context that this book must be considered. There are many common threads in our profession, and academic, public, school and special librarians share a common rich heritage. Much of what is done in special libraries is done in all libraries, and this book does not deal with any of these common issues. There are excellent books that describe such basic professional concerns, and no attempt is made here to replicate other work. This work is also not a primer for a neophyte who has suddenly been thrust into an operational role in a special library. It is particularly not for those individuals who have no background in librarianship at all, and whose promotion may have come "from the ranks." There are other books that can serve as introductions to self-training. I do not want to repeat their content—nor am I sure I want to do anything to encourage and support the process or the practice.

This book is aimed primarily at individuals who are already special librarians and who have not had the opportunity to contemplate what they do and why they do it. It is also aimed at other librarians who are interested in this field and might want to consider making a lateral career change. Finally, it is aimed at library and information science school students, particularly those at the master's level. It represents the curriculum developed over a period of eight years of teaching a course in special librarianship and information centers, and it should prove useful as a textbook.

However, a warning to teachers is in order. This book assumes that the student already has at least a basic understanding of librarianship as a profession as it is conveyed in most educational institutions through a core curriculum dealing with reference, collection development, materials analysis and organizational philosophy. While the book deals with these areas in the special library context, it makes no attempt to define basic terms. It assumes they are understood.

The book is, as clearly stated in the title, a book on management. The text will make the reasons for this strategy clear. Special librarians differ from other librarians primarily because of the settings in which they work and because of the larger organizational value systems to which they must adapt. Special librarians operate in environments in which the need for a library is not always assumed, as it would be in an academic or public library relationship. They work under constraints of time and space that are usually greater than those encountered by other librarians, and under financial constraints that may not be greater but that are certainly different.

Special libraries frequently have no recognized rationale for existence except in terms of what they can accomplish for others. The pragmatism of this profession is beautifully captured in the Special Libraries Association slogan "Putting Knowledge to Work," which has served the association without modification for more than a half century, through a succession of techniques and technologies.

The book is a management book because ultimately how a special library fares depends not only on how well it performs, but how it demonstrates its contribution and fights for attention and resources in an environment in which nothing is assumed. This can be a risk, and it is not for the fainthearted. It is also an opportunity for those prepared to grasp at opportunities. Special librarians, like other librarians, have no natural enemies. Libraries are still perceived as having positive qualities, and that is clearly an advantage. The special librarian's greatest danger is not his or her enemies. It is indifference from those who don't know a good library from a bad one. Even if they knew, they would probably only care to the extent to which such a difference affected their own work and their progression. The special library's unique enemy is not opposition. It is indifference. It is trivialization. These are the attitudes that must be fought.

Ultimately, any book which seeks to examine characteristics and situations that make special librarians "special" can be at best an approximation, and it is presented with that caveat to the reader. All special librarians must and do define the profession in their own terms. That they have been able to do this and find a basis for meaningful recognition, communication and camaraderie despite their many differences is what made this book worth writing.

Two final comments must be made. The book makes no attempt at bibliographic completeness or even bibliographic adequacy. While there are suggested further readings at the end of each chapter, and a combined bibliography at the end of the book, the titles are indicative and highly selective. There is a great deal written about specific issues and problems in special librarianship. Special librarians more than others exchange ideas in the published literature, at conferences and in informal gatherings. The reader interested in following up on any topic in greater depth should consult one of the bibliographic tools. He or she should be warned that much of the writing is not cool and dispassionate. It is filled with the urgency, exhortation and zeal that so characterize the field.

I gratefully acknowledge a debt to *Special Libraries: A Guide for Management*, Second Edition. This booklet, edited by Janet Ahrensfeld, Elin Christianson and David King, and published in 1981 by the Special Libraries Association, is full of succinct, useful information, and I have drawn on its incisive and well-articulated arguments as a teacher, lecturer and author of this book.

—Herbert S. White
January 1984

1

What Are Special Libraries and Information Centers?

The question of what special libraries are, and by extension what they are not, must obviously be addressed by anyone who seeks to deal with criteria for managing them. However, although it appears a very simple question, it is a very elusive one.

ATTEMPTS TO DEFINE SPECIAL LIBRARIES

There have been a number of attempts to define special libraries, but they are generally neither specific nor comprehensive enough to be adequate.

Libraries with Specialized Clientele and Materials

It has been suggested that special libraries are those that deal with a specialized clientele or with specialized materials or with a combination of both. Such a definition may appear helpful at first glance, but examination quickly indicates that it is far from satisfactory. Under those terms any library quickly qualifies as a special library. Certainly school libraries would meet both parts of the definition. They deal with a specialized clientele (students) and with specialized materials (those appropriate to a school setting). All university libraries would also qualify as special libraries, as would public libraries, as soon as it is recognized that the user population in an urban ethnic neighborhood differs substantially from that in a small farming community. It is therefore clear that such distinctions will not serve us in the attempt to determine what is "special" about special libraries.

Libraries with Special Librarians

It has been suggested, perhaps with more serious intent than might be assumed, that a special librarian is anyone who states that he or she is one, and by implication that the libraries they serve are special libraries. Since the professional associations that are commonly considered as dealing with special libraries have no test of credentials or qualifying examination, it is certainly true that anyone who wants to call himself or herself a special librarian can do so without fear of contradiction or confrontation.

Special Libraries Association Membership

The fact that many individuals do this can be seen from an analysis of recent membership patterns within the Special Libraries Association (SLA), the largest and most prominent of the professional bodies. This shows that 55% of the members of the Association are employed in corporate libraries or other areas of the for-profit sector. This is the group directly and most immediately identified with special librarianship for most other librarians and the general public. However, while this is by far the largest group, it comprises only a little more than half of the total of SLA members. This group itself contains many differences in emphasis, such as support of scientific research and development, manufacturing, banks, insurance, and advertising and marketing.

The second largest group, 22%, works in government libraries, and here again there are many variations. Government installations exist at the federal, state and municipal levels, and range from laboratories that develop and test military hardware to libraries that serve preschool children on overseas military bases. At a Veterans Administration hospital, it would not be unusual for one library to serve the needs of both medical researchers and patients seeking recreational reading materials. For simplicity of compilation, this group also includes librarians in some quasi-governmental not-for-profit organizations such as historical societies and art museums. A further 13% work in academic libraries, usually, but not always, in departmentalized collections in major academic institutions. A final 10% are employed in public libraries, and for them the same distinction can usually, but not always, be applied.

However, type of library is not the only way in which special librarians categorize and fragment themselves. The Special Libraries Association, in itself only one of a number of organizations that speak for the profession, is partitioned into 29 divisions, which primarily represent subject interests. Some of these are further subdivided into sections. A mere listing, without comment, of the 29 SLA divisions will suffice to underscore the diversity and complexity:

Advertising and Marketing	Museums-Arts-Humanities
Aerospace	Natural Resources
Biological Sciences	Newspapers
Business and Finance	Nuclear Science
Chemistry	Petroleum and Energy Resources
Education	Pharmaceutical
Engineering	Physics-Astronomy-Mathematics
Environmental Information	Picture
Food and Nutrition	Public Utilities
Geography and Map	Publishing
Information Technology	Science-Technology
Insurance and Employee Benefits	Social Science
Library Management	Telecommunication
Metal/Materials	Transportation
Military Librarians	

By the time this is read, there may be more than 29 divisions. Based on historical patterns, there certainly won't be fewer.

Membership in Other Associations

Membership in the Special Libraries Association is certainly not the only indication of an interest in special libraries. SLA, founded in 1909, now has about 12,000 members. The even older Medical Library Association, founded in 1898, has a robust 5000; the American Society for Information Science, which makes a claim to bridging the gap between librarianship and information technology, enrolls another 4000 or so. The American Association of Law Libraries, founded in 1906 and thus also older than SLA, lists about 3500 members, and a variety of other "special" library associations, ranging from music to theater to theology, add at least several thousand more. The total begins to approach and perhaps surpass that of the American Library Association (ALA), founded in 1876, and with about 37,000 members as of 1983. At times ALA claims to speak for the library profession at large, a statement that may be based more on bravado than substance when it is further realized that the various specialized associations are growing at a more rapid rate. (Of course, many librarians are members of more than one association, making precise numerical comparisons impractical.)

Even within ALA there are many specialized associations, with separate publications and conferences. These include separate groupings for public, school, and college and research librarians, as well as groups from all of these settings for individuals with particular interests—for example, information technology and its applications. Those who follow ALA's organizational politics have noted a consistently growing demand for autonomy and flexibility, which may lead to a repetition of the breakaway that created the Medical and Special Libraries Associations. This would then force us to redefine the profession as a group of federated or allied specializations, with some common interests and many separate ones. There are certainly role models for such a structure in both the American Federation of Information Processing Societies and the American Institute of Physics, both of which encompass a variety of large and small separate organizations. However, at least for the moment there is little impetus for such a change in librarianship.

Libraries Offering Special Service

There are some who would not quarrel with the suggestion that all librarians are in fact special librarians, and some who would enthusiastically embrace the suggestion that all *good* librarians are special librarians, in that they deal with each user and each need as though it were separate and special. Neophyte reference librarians are taught to do this in library education programs, although pressures of workloads sometimes force them to take shortcuts. It probably cannot be denied that the literature of self-professed special librarians carries the implication not only of being different but of being better. Many see themselves as an elite group working under greater pressures and toward the solution of more significant problems.

Such comparisons are both self-serving and unfair. Quality of library service is not predicated on the type of organization or the management reporting mechanism. This

writer knows of some industrial librarians whose level of information service is characterized not only by passivity but almost by service avoidance, and he knows some grade
school librarians who have succeeded in developing individually interactive information
centers that have fourth graders as clients.

THE INFORMATION CENTER

Descriptions of organizations being served, of the quality of that service, of the existence or absence of computer equipment, and of the title of the service group all serve
imperfectly to define or describe special libraries, although they may lead us to situations
of greater probability. Even further confusion is caused by the introduction of the term
"information center," a development largely of the last 20 years. It was assumed then, and
often still is, that information centers differ from libraries in dealing more extensively with
"nontraditional" materials such as reports, memoranda, inventory records, production figures, and engineering and personnel files, as opposed to books and periodicals. It was also
suggested that information centers would take a greater responsibility in the subject analysis of the collection and in the use of computers and other advanced technologies for the
establishment of communication links. These assumptions are at best generalizations; there
is no philosophical difference between what an information center always does and what a
library can or should be allowed to do.

While information centers generally suggest a greater degree of aggressive service and
technological sophistication, this may or may not be true. Corporations such as Bell
Laboratories feel quite comfortable performing advanced and sophisticated information
functions in organizations called libraries. Some so-called information centers are nothing
more than clerically staffed document warehouses. Some librarians have found it expedient
to adopt a new nomenclature, in part because the word "library" suggests for some users a
passive and nonresponsive organization from their youth or from media advertising. Many
librarians have made the change eagerly, anxious to shed a stereotyped image. Others have
done so with nostalgia and regret. They would prefer to be librarians but find the communications barrier too difficult to hurdle.

Nomenclature changes, whether to information center, information resources center,
technical information management center or others limited only by the innovative ability
of planners, have been most prevalent in industrial, business and governmental settings,
but assumptions of what the name implies must be approached with considerable caution.
As some cynics have stated, the clearest difference between a library manager and the
manager of an information center may be about $5000 in annual salary. This book will use
the terms interchangeably.

SIGNIFICANT CHARACTERISTICS OF SPECIAL LIBRARIES

For the purposes of this book, none of these stated generalizations about what consti-
tutes a special library or information center are very useful. We will have to find our own
definitions of the characteristics likely to differentiate special libraries—recognizing their
own diversity—from other libraries that we would not consider special or that would not

consider themselves special. Clearly, these will also be generalizations, but they may be more recognizable and applicable. The first five characteristics listed below are stated very effectively in the SLA publication *Special Libraries: A Guide for Management*, Second Edition, and are adapted for this list. The rest arise from this writer's own observations as a special librarian and information manager, from the literature of the field and from conversations with others.

EMPHASIS ON PROVIDING INFORMATION

Special libraries emphasize the function of providing information. This distinction is an important one and will be dealt with more fully at the end of this chapter and in other chapters. Providing information is not the primary function of most libraries. For example, libraries housed in educational institutions are primarily responsible for supporting the learning process. Library users are not necessarily provided information; rather, they are given tools so that they can find their own information, and ultimately whether or not they find it is their own problem. There are also librarians who will argue that their task is the development of a collection. Whether or not material is located or is accessible when needed is something they do not consider their problem.

Other libraries exist for recreational or aesthetic purposes, or because it is assumed that the parent body's scholarly pursuits (or appearance) require the existence of a strong library collection. (It should be noted that the existence of a strong library collection, and of a highly qualified library staff, are not necessarily complementary goals. In times of budgetary constraints they may become adversarial objectives, as many academic librarians well know.)

By contrast, the function of the special library is in general the provision of information, frequently for immediate and utilitarian purposes. Where it comes from does not really matter.

NONTRADITIONAL SETTINGS

Special libraries are found where other types of libraries often are not. While academic and public librarians, particularly in department collections, may consider theirs a special library, the setting is nevertheless traditional. Business and industrial libraries invariably are found in places where no library was planned or expected. Because of this they can be found in settings that might be considered unusual, such as the 38th floor of a high-rise office building or in the corner of a manufacturing plant.

A LIMITED BODY OF USERS

Special libraries usually serve a limited body of users, with the limitation established by considerations other than the library's. Public and academic libraries provide services and materials to anyone who stands at the desk and asks for attention. Access to special libraries is frequently limited by organizational concerns of security and sensitivity, and outsiders may not be allowed. As a result special librarians know who their users are, or at least who their potential users might be.

LIMITED SUBJECT SCOPE

Special libraries are limited in subject scope. Since the service clientele is finite and its needs at least somewhat predictable, special library collections are usually intensive and limited. There is generally no expectation that the collection should provide books of poetry to employees in an engineering firm, since these individuals also share generally available access to public and academic libraries.

SMALL COLLECTIONS

Special library collections are frequently very small. Limitations of clientele and of subject scope lead quite naturally to smaller collections and staffs. Additional reasons, to be discussed later, involve the fact that the decision to fund the special library is made within the context of "real money" budgetary alternatives. Many special libraries, perhaps close to half, operate with only one or two professional staff members. Libraries and information centers with a professional staff of a dozen or more are very rare indeed. By contrast, some academic and public library systems include more than 100 professionals.

INCONSPICUOUS QUARTERS

Special libraries are often inconspicuously housed. Since these libraries are frequently for internal use, there is no perceived need to provide a showplace with which to impress outside visitors. (If such a value system does exist, librarians can of course take advantage of it.) Also, special libraries, unlike public or academic libraries, do not occupy buildings that have been especially provided for them. They share space in a highly competitive environment with other organizational groups usually also in great need of more room—and with partitions that can be easily moved. It goes without saying that space in the Empire State Building or the Sears Tower is a not insignificant expense and inspires vigorous competition.

THE NEED TO ESTABLISH USEFULNESS

Special libraries are not viewed as self-evidently good. Special libraries tend to be supported by people if they find them useful and for no other reason. By contrast, public, academic and school libraries are supported for the presumed good of the community. Public libraries are generally supported for use by "other people's kids"; academic libraries are perceived as crucial to the quality of the university even by those who never set foot in them; and school libraries, like schools in general, are supported by all taxpayers, sometimes with the backing of a federal judge. This is a crucial difference, which places considerable additional pressures on the special library, and which will be explored in greater detail in later chapters.

RELATIONSHIP TO ORGANIZATIONAL MISSION

Special libraries support, but are not integral to, the purpose of the organization in which they are housed. Libraries in educational institutions, be they school or academic, share the overall mission of the parent body. Public libraries usually assume a general support for their own mission in education, culture and recreation, although they sometimes find during periods of budgetary crunch that this assumption may lack understanding and support.

Special librarians, by contrast, tend to have no such illusions. Manufacturing corporations, banks, professional associations and government agencies have objectives in which libraries play no *directly discernible* part. The libraries may not be opposed, but they will be supported only to the extent to which a contribution to the overall mission (e.g., manufacturing automobiles to produce a profit for the stockholders) is perceived. By contrast, even subject departments in public and academic libraries, which share many of the characteristics of other special libraries in terms of user and collection specialization, nevertheless have protection under the umbrella of the general institutional mission.

MANAGEMENT THAT IS NOT LIBRARY-ORIENTED

Special libraries frequently report to individuals who have no interest in or understanding of them. Public library boards and academic library committees are largely self-selected and dedicated individuals who have offered to participate because they have an interest in the success of the library and because they care about its mission. At a minimum, they care about how well they are personally served. In academia, the role of the library in achieving prestige and recognition for the institution is understood and accepted.

By contrast, assignment of management responsibilities involving libraries in corporations and government installations is frequently a matter of arbitrary choice. The librarian's manager may or may not be pleased at the assignment, but in any case it is not likely that he or she was chosen because of any particular knowledge of libraries. This clearly affects the communication process.

THE IMPACT OF ORGANIZATIONAL POLICIES

Special libraries are subject to overall organizational policies. Many if not most public and academic libraries are separately housed, with their own job titles and salary structures and with personnel selection procedures devised by the librarians. By contrast, special librarians tend to be a small part of a larger organizational whole, with personnel procedures, job descriptions, wage and salary policies, and accounting procedures already in place. Some adaptation or modification is possible, but by and large the special library must operate within the framework in which it already finds itself.

UNTRAINED CLIENTELE

Special libraries frequently deal with untrained clientele. Most other libraries (except perhaps for school libraries) deal with self-selected users. They are interested, or they wouldn't be there at all. If they are not yet trained to self-sufficiency, repeated exposure quickly prepares them, and those not interested in the process weed themselves from the user group.

Special librarians also have some of these clients, but to a much greater extent they must deal with individuals who are there by necessity and not by choice. Even more importantly, special librarians concerned about growth and even survival of their organizations must seek ways to serve individuals who, left to their own resources, would not be there at all. For this reason, limits imposed within the organization must be examined carefully. Yours may be chartered as a library to serve Research and Development, but if there is no other library then you must seek to extend service to all of the other areas of the organization as well.

WORKING UNDER TIME PRESSURES

Special librarians operate under considerable time pressures. In fact, this characteristic is most often singled out by special librarians. Users of special libraries often operate under extreme time pressures—tomorrow's report deadline or this afternoon's meeting. Basic research over the span of a lifetime, not unusual in academia, is virtually nonexistent in organizations served by special libraries. Unfortunate as it may seem, information provided on time and within cost constraints usually takes precedence over complete—and sometimes even over accurate—information.

Other libraries have historically measured the quality of their service in quantitative terms—size of collection for academic libraries, circulation for public libraries. Neither of these statistics has any significance in the organization that houses the special library, and this distinction should be kept in mind.

Another reminder of time constraints comes from the writings and speeches of Calvin Mooers, an early pioneer in information work. Mooers has postulated that in an environment in which it is known that information is available, but in which it is difficult, cumbersome or time-consuming to acquire it, individuals will make assumptions and guesses and pretend there is no information available.

LIBRARIES THAT TAKE ON THE USER'S BURDEN

Special libraries are not self-service institutions—at least they should not be. In an educational environment, teaching the student how to find the answer to tomorrow's question for himself is considered more important than convenience or if necessary even accuracy with regard to today's question. In special libraries, today's question is the only question that matters. Moreover, many special library users are not particularly interested in pursuing their own information research or in learning how to do it. They would rather simply leave the problem and proceed to something else while the library staff fills in the gaps. It is a phenomenon which Grieg Aspnes, an innovative special librarian and former president of the Special Libraries Association, has referred to as "assuming the tension of the situation from the user, or... lifting the burden from the user's back."

It must be recognized that this suggested treatment of users is framed as a generalization. Some users like doing their own literature searching, enjoy browsing through the stacks waiting for serendipity to strike, prefer to sit at the terminal accessing data bases.

Some, but not many. Others do it themselves because they perceive an unwillingness on the librarian's part or because their background in academic institutions has prepared them for such an unwillingness. Others don't know the librarians and don't trust their expertise.

Users must be dealt with at the level of their own preference. It is possible that, as some have been predicting for many years, we are entering an age of self-service information access with individuals preferring to search at their personal terminals. It is possible, but there is as yet no indication that it is true. Online access systems designed for direct use by professionals are largely still used by information specialists, librarians and information intermediaries.

The important thing to recall is that in the special library situation there is no moral issue at stake. Furthermore, it is generally true that things that can be done by the librarian should be done by the librarian, not by the user. The librarian is more skilled at the process, and the user has other things to do. Finally, and unfortunately, the user is probably drawing a higher salary, and his or her time is therefore considered more valuable.

SPECIALIZED AND INTERNAL MATERIALS

Special libraries frequently deal with specialized and internal materials. Public libraries primarily deal with books, academic libraries with books and periodicals. Techniques for dealing with these have been highly developed in the profession. Shared cataloging through Library of Congress cards and OCLC terminals, union lists and journal indexes are tools available to any librarian.

Special librarians use these generally available publications as well, but to a much greater extent they must deal with reports, memoranda, specifications, laboratory notebooks and vendor catalogs. What other libraries frequently relegate to the uncataloged purgatory of the vertical files is for many special librarians the lifeblood of the collection. In some aerospace libraries technical reports may outnumber books by more than 40 to 1.

These documents usually have a high degree of currency; they may rapidly become obsolete. They must be made available quickly, and because outside analytical services are frequently lacking, whatever analysis takes place must be provided within the special library. This is particularly true with regard to sensitive internal documents, which in some special libraries are the most heavily used.

RESTRICTED ACCESS

Special libraries frequently have restricted access. As has already been pointed out, special libraries exist to serve the larger mission of the organization in which they are housed. Depending on what that mission is, access by outsiders may be severely limited. This would certainly be less true for a historical society library than for an engineering company attempting to protect its designs from the eyes of competitors. Some organizations even consider the list of journals holdings to be sensitive, because it discloses areas of research concentration. Other libraries feel sensitive about what they borrow through interlibrary loan, for the same reason. Finally, in addition to proprietary data and internal files, there may be constraints of government security, for those organizations working on projects of this kind.

All of these limitations are important and must be maintained. At the same time, they create difficulties for special librarians, who from viewpoints of both principle and pragmatism prefer to share information as widely as possible. Special librarians do cooperate and share, probably more than other kinds of librarians. How and why are questions to be discussed later in this book.

ENTREPRENEURIAL OPPORTUNITIES

Special librarians usually have fewer constraints on how they do what they do. The preceding characteristics may have appeared to the reader as limitations and restrictions. This last one definitely is not. It has already been pointed out that the special library operates in organizations that are neither knowledgeable about what special libraries do nor particularly anxious to find out. This largely frees special librarians from frequently well-meaning but usually intrusive controls from adminstrators or committees, which are often more policy-oriented than advisory. By and large, the organizational management housing the special library is concerned with levels of expenditure and—one hopes—with levels of service. It is rarely concerned with the details of how things are accomplished, as long as the results are satisfactory. This provides one important level of freedom.

Another comes, at least potentially, from the fact that few organizations with special libraries have any idea of the appropriate level of support and expenditure. The guidelines for support so clearly exchanged among academic administrators, and generally available to public officials who want to find out, are rarely known in the special library environment. This certainly does not mean that the management which supports special libraries is anxious to spend more money. Far from it. The lack of supporting data for the correctness of present levels of operational support can and sometimes does lead to a reduction of support below that which would be tolerated if "reasonable" comparisons were available. In fact, at times reductions can continue to the point where extinction becomes the logical next step, as James M. Matarazzo has pointed out.

However, the absence of information in this area can serve as an opportunity as well as a threat, and many special librarians have used that opportunity to build levels of service far beyond what their managements might have approved had they known what was "reasonable." In other words, special librarianship, probably unlike any other branches of the profession, is at least potentially entrepreneurial in nature. It is a field ideally suited to innovators and to risk takers. It equally clearly is not for everyone.

LIMITATIONS AND EXCEPTIONS

It will be noted that the characterizations and definitions above exclude libraries served by some of the most prominent members of the governance structure of associations representing special libraries. This exclusion affects particularly academic librarians, and to some extent public librarians, and it is not intended as any sort of slight or insult. The point is simply that a specialized collection of materials in a university or public library, no matter how excellently organized or aggressively used, nevertheless operates within the broader management and decision framework, and is available to users who deal with that library as part of the academic or public whole.

As such, those libraries fail many of the tests which this chapter has established. For example, such libraries are most certainly viewed as self-evidently good things to have. That is an important distinction between the chemistry professor and the industrial chemist, between the business executive's support of a public library with tax funds and of his own corporate library out of what would otherwise be greater profits. Of course, the distinctions are not always as clear as stated above, and both exceptions and fuzzy demarcations can be seen. However, in the continuing attempt to concentrate on characteristics that make special libraries special or different, some arbitrariness is necessary.

INFORMATION VERSUS DOCUMENTS

One final point must be made here. When we have spoken of information, we invariably mean documents that contain information. For academic and public librarians, these are usually more formal documents such as books, considered "worthy" of full bibliographic control and treatment. Most special libraries deal with far more relaxed definitions: reports, pamphlets and memoranda may be placed under more complete bibliographic control. Nevertheless, we are still dealing primarily with finite documents rather than with information, which is more likely to exist as it is really needed in portions of a variety of documents and files. Much of the transaction between librarian and user in special libraries deals with documents in part because many users come from academic and public backgrounds and have no inkling of any other form of transaction.

Some special librarians are beginning to move toward a communication process that deals in information and not documents, because there is ample evidence that users who trust you will prefer greater specificity to save their own time. Even beyond the horizon of information lies the provision of evaluated information. Later chapters will deal with some of these issues.

THE REWARDS OF SPECIAL LIBRARIANSHIP

The special libraries profession is one which its practitioners would certainly characterize as challenging and demanding—and perhaps even as pressured. At the same time, they would argue that there are rewards and benefits. The most immediate of these comes from the fact that special librarians tend to be closer to the end use of their work and can therefore see the results of their efforts. Occasionally, users and managers can see and appreciate them as well. Special librarians tend to work in an area that, although certainly susceptible to economic fluctuations, has tended to grow more rapidly than the library profession as a whole. They work in organizations whose policies with regard to salaries, benefits and professional support are frequently more generous than those in the academic or public sector, although those advantages are rarely passed along to the librarian automatically. They work hours usually more attuned to a business schedule, and evening and weekend work is rare except under special circumstances.

Most importantly, however, successful special librarians find it exhilarating to work in an environment where they can clearly see the results of their activities, and in which recognition and status are not automatically foreclosed by others' preconceptions. They are entrepreneurs and risk takers who like to have the opportunity to help shape their own destinies.

SUGGESTED ADDITIONAL READINGS

Christianson, Elin and Janet L. Ahrensfeld. "Toward a Better Understanding of New Special Libraries." *Special Libraries* 71:146-153 (March 1980).

Drake, Miriam A. "The Management of Libraries as Professional Organizations." *Special Libraries* 68:181-186 (May/June 1977).

Drucker, Peter F. "Managing the Public Service Institution." *College & Research Libraries* 37:4-14 (January 1976).

Hull, David and Henry D. Feamley. "The Museum Library in the United States: A Sample." *Special Libraries* 67:289-298 (July 1976).

Matarazzo, James M. *Closing the Corporate Library: Case Studies on the Decision Making Process*. New York: Special Libraries Association, 1981.

Pizer, Irwin. "Biomedical Libraries." *Special Libraries* 69:296-299 (August 1978).

Severson-Tris, Mary A. "The Map Library in Private Industry." *Special Libraries* 69:94-99 (March 1978).

Special Libraries: A Guide for Management, Second Edition. New York: Special Libraries Association, 1981.

Steuermann, Clara. "Music Libraries." *Special Libraries* 69:425-428 (November 1978).

Waldron, Helen J. "The Business of Running a Special Library." *Special Libraries* 62:63-70 (February 1971).

Walker, William B. "Art Libraries: International and Interdisciplinary." *Special Libraries* 69:476-481 (December 1978).

White, Herbert S. "An American Federation of Library Associations: The Time Has Come." *Library Journal* 107:860-864 (May 1, 1982).

2

Evolution and Development

The development of special libraries, as this book considers them, is a phenomenon of the 20th century. Because they are so new, it is particularly remarkable that the 1983 *American Library Directory* (published by R.R. Bowker Co.) suggests that 33.4% of all U.S. libraries are special libraries, a number surpassed only by public libraries and almost double the number of academic libraries.

Even these statistics are conservative, both as an actual count and as a projection. Nobody really knows how many special libraries there are, both because there is no automatic process by which a staffed collection of materials reaches "official" status, and because corporate organizations are not obliged to report their libraries at all. The *American Library Directory* figure of 9703 special libraries (including armed forces, government, medical, law and religious) is a count of known libraries that are uncovered through the listing techniques employed by the publisher. Others have suggested that the actual number of special libraries is almost twice as great. If this is true, then special libraries would have become, in less than 100 years, the most populous form of library organization.

Even if that assertion is not yet true, conservative projections would soon make it true. The number of special libraries grows at an average of 5% per year, while at present and for the foreseeable future both academic and public library growth is expected to remain at best flat. Therefore, even accepting the conservative published numbers, it would only be 1992 when the number of special libraries exceeded the number of public libraries. Back in 1928, the noted historian and political scientist Frederic Austin Ogg wrote in a survey report to the American Council of Learned Societies, "The growth of special libraries is the outstanding feature of library history in the past twenty years." Forty years later Jesse Shera, dean of the School of Library and Information Science at Case Western Reserve University, characterized the 20th century as "the era of special libraries and specialized services." The years since Shera's statement have done nothing to contradict either assertion.

WHERE DO SPECIAL LIBRARIES FLOURISH?

At the same time, it would be inaccurate to describe the development of special libraries as a worldwide phenomenon. The development of special libraries hinges in large part on societal changes: industrialization; the development of rapid communications techniques; the emergence of what has been identified as the information society, or the post-industrial society; and the growth of service professions. They all amount to the same thing, because they depend on a willingness for and ultimately an insistence on the provision of information resources, as well as on an economic mechanism to support such decisions.

Special libraries do not flourish in what has broadly been termed the "German traditional academic environment," in which scholars insist on taking all responsibility for the development and use of collections and are willing to delegate only the most routine and mundane clerical duties. Such a perception—libraries controlled not by librarians and information specialists but by their users—still characterizes much of American academia, and special librarianship cannot survive and grow in such an environment. It exists to a much greater extent in some other industrialized nations where the management of libraries is still something scholars do in their spare time. There is, in such an environment, no real acceptance of librarianship as a profession separate from the scholarship of chemistry, philosophy, history or other academic disciplines.

On the other hand, in the many countries in which the economy is controlled and all decisions are made by a centralized government, all libraries are government libraries, and all libraries are fundamentally the same, be they public, academic or what might be labeled as special.

Special libraries tend to flourish in organizations in which accuracy, efficiency and timeliness have a recognized and usually tangible value and reward. It is therefore no accident that the development of special libraries began with the industrial revolution. It was accelerated by an evolving scarcity of resources, which put an emphasis on competitive efficiency. The movement has taken its greatest stimulus from the growth of both information sources and an interdisciplinary need to access them, which has outstripped the ability of scholars to keep up with the literature of their own field, let alone allied fields. The success of special libraries appears directly related to the ability of its professionals to make this point and the willingness of users to accept it.

Special libraries exist in their most highly developed form in the United States and Canada. There is also a strong historic special library tradition in Great Britain. Other industrialized nations with uncontrolled economies, including West Germany, France, the Scandinavian countries, Japan, Taiwan and some Latin American nations, are moving toward special librarianship. The Special Libraries Association (SLA) now has three Canadian chapters and one European chapter. The American Society for Information Science

(ASIS) also has chapters in Canada and in northern Europe, despite the fact that separate national associations exist in these regions. ASIS also has a chapter based in Taipei in the Republic of China.

THE ORIGINS OF SPECIAL LIBRARIES

Most library historians would agree that the special library movement had its beginning in libraries serving government agencies and professional associations in the 18th and 19th centuries. In particular, early legal and medical collections to support professional training date in the United States from the 18th century. Scientific and historical societies also established libraries during this period; some of these, in the United States and particularly in England, had collections that could be considered excellent for their times. It was also a time of the development of private library collections, which were the interest and often the consuming passion of wealthy and educated individuals, and which they made available to their friends and colleagues.

The development of some social libraries, and of mechanics' and mercantile libraries during the latter half of the 19th century, is considered by some to be the forerunner of today's special library, but the connection is tenuous at best. These libraries were general collections with a social or educational purpose; they were staffed by volunteers or employees with no particular training, or by educated scholars or laymen who were carrying out these activities as a hobby or in addition to other duties.

The climate for special libraries began to change in the United States after 1876. At this time, libraries in general were receiving a greater degree of attention and concern, with pressures for the establishment of public libraries and for the preparation of individuals to staff them. More particularly, as Elin Christianson has pointed out, the development of special libraries was affected by growth in business and industry, and the emerging recognition that the organization with a good collection and access to its contents might have a competitive advantage over other organizations in the same business field. The pragmatic and nonidealistic evaluation of library and information services, which so deeply characterizes special libraries and which is a focus of much of this book, came very early indeed!

SLA: THE EARLY YEARS

In addition, some public librarians, including John Cotton Dana of the Newark Free Library, revered as the founding spirit of the Special Libraries Association but claimed by other library specializations as well, saw very quickly the importance of providing business with information services from the urban public library. In 1909, in a meeting at Bretton Woods, NH, 20 librarians representing largely public libraries and commercial organizations met to lay the groundwork for the formation of SLA. The first conference, held in New York City in the fall of that year, attracted 40 member participants, and 56 names were ultimately inscribed as charter members. Dana was elected as first president.

Although the membership included a diverse range of state and federal agencies, nonprofit associations, and business firms and leagues, the largest group came from the public library sector. This initial diversity has of course continued, despite the reduction of public library emphasis and its replacement with a greater representation from the for-profit sector, particularly in science and technology.

The factors that caused these pioneers to gather are difficult to isolate. Without doubt each individual had his or her own reasons. However, there was a general dissatisfaction with representation of their needs and interests by the American Library Association, founded in 1876, and perceived then and perhaps now as dominated by the interests of academic and large public libraries. Special librarians were of course not the first to act on that dissatisfaction. As noted in Chapter 1, medical librarians had broken away from ALA in 1898 to form the Association of Medical Librarians, and the American Association of Law Libraries had been formed under similar circumstances in 1906.

A Wide Range of Interests

However, the Special Libraries Association was the first to attempt organization across broad subject lines and to concern itself with concepts of information service to business, industry and government, independent of subject scope. It is this very diversity that characterizes SLA to this day and differentiates it from organizations of law librarians, which deal primarily with law schools and law firms, or from groups of medical librarians, who concentrate either on medical research or on hospitals.

Special librarians continue to represent what has now become an even wider range of interests and specializations. At one point, successive presidents of SLA were from the New York Metropolitan Museum of Art, IBM, General Motors, the U.S. Air Force Air University Library (AL), the pharmaceuticals industry, an advertising agency and the Canadian government. Little did the early special library pioneers realize that they had carved out for themselves the most dynamic and rapidly growing sector of the information spectrum.

ALA-SLA Relationships

It is not recorded whether officials of the American Library Association expressed concern or fear at those defections in the early 1900s. In all probability, their reaction may have been one of hurt bewilderment. ALA has always felt, and has consistently represented in Congressional testimony, that it represents the entire library profession, increasingly inaccurate as such an assumption has become. As noted earlier, ALA now faces similar pressures for independent action and organization from groups of academic, public and other librarians, and this will undoubtedly continue as long as individuals insist on communing in the smallest group of people with similar interests for which organization is possible. If SLA has succeeded and grown, it is because it has recognized this concept and allowed, by and large, both the forestry and the picture librarians in its midst to do what suits them, without ensnaring them in organizational red tape.

Regardless of the reactions ALA bureaucrats may have had, the ensuing decades caused relatively little concern or fear. Special libraries in the years following World War I were affected by the growing impact of industrialization and the greater development of technical libraries, as differentiated from the business libraries, which had formed the initial nucleus of corporate membership. Nevertheless, growth was slow, and the financial health of the Association fragile at best. Most if not all of the work was done by volunteers, setting a pattern for volunteerism that exists throughout librarianship, and particularly special librarianship, to this day.

By the mid-1920s there was some concern about the survival of the Special Libraries Association, and reaffiliation with the American Library Association was considered. The talks did not succeed, and both bodies limped, together with the rest of the country, through the depression of the 1930s. Despite its constraints, SLA had managed to start two major projects now in commercial hands—the Public Affairs Information Service and the Artisans Trade Index, which later became the Industrial Arts Index and is now the Applied Science and Technology Index.

ASSOCIATIONS IN OTHER COUNTRIES

The British Association of Special Libraries and Information Bureaux (ASLIB) was formed in 1924. Unlike its United States counterpart, ASLIB had slightly greater stability of funding, since its early efforts were underwritten in part by grants from the Carnegie United Kingdom Trust. It has differed from the Special Libraries Association in a number of significant ways, including its emphasis on organizational rather than individual membership and its greater reliance on research activities, to a large extent supported by government grants and the sale of publications.

As noted earlier, special library organizations in other industrialized countries have developed much later and to some extent are still overcoming their more recent trends toward industrialization and, even more importantly, the reluctance to grant professional status to librarians and information specialists. In Eastern Europe and other countries with controlled economies, no real comparison is possible, because librarians may deal with specialized collections and even geographically identified users, but operate under the same organizational constraints as all other libraries.

WORLD WAR II AND AFTER

Special libraries were profoundly affected by World War II and by the changes in the types of information and the attitudes toward information generated by this conflict. World War II, unlike all preceding wars, was a technological war, fought not in the trenches through massed cavalry and infantry charges but through technological sophistication. The Axis development of rockets and the Allied development of bombsights, radar and atomic weapons were triumphs of science and technology. These in turn were heavily reliant on rapid and accurate scientific and technical communications, in huge quantities.

Dependence on traditional methods of communication through books and journals—estimated by William Garvey to take anywhere from five to eight years between the development of an idea and its communication to others—was recognized very early to be totally unsatisfactory. This is a significant point, and a difference that characterizes special libraries, as contrasted to academic and public libraries, to this day. Monographs are a relatively small and insignificant portion of many special library collections, because the information they contain is old, frequently outdated and therefore primarily only useful for broad and general background.

This point was quickly understood by Vannevar Bush, appointed to head the National Defense Research Committee Office of Scientific Research and Development. Bush urged heavy use of the technical report, an easily produced and reproduced (usually carbon or mimeograph) document, which was not edited and could appear within days or weeks and then be mailed directly in multiple copies. It was an early form of selective dissemination of information, although the emphasis was on dissemination rather than on selectivity. Given the pressures of the war effort, it was undoubtedly a pragmatically correct decision.

As World War II ended, there was a tremendous upsurge in scientific and technical development, born from the development of shortages through six years of war, from the need to rebuild large devastated areas and from the ability to apply to civilian uses a whole array of sophisticated technologies developed for the military. In addition, the new professionals of this technology, and the users of the information generated and needed by it, were largely weaned on and used to the new techniques of rapid and informal communication, and they were fully prepared to continue what had worked for them in the past. It was a development for which most of librarianship, wedded to slow but careful bibliographic examination of major works, was totally unprepared—and to some extent still is.

It was largely a combination of these factors, together with the growth of electronic techniques for the handling of documents, which gave rise to the development of new kinds of library and information service collections. These were immediately—both by their very nature and by their pragmatic service approach to the types of materials and needs of users—special libraries, whether they were recognized as such or not.

The tremendous growth of special libraries in the two decades following World War II was in the field of scientific and technical information and concentrated in both the commercial and the governmental sectors. The emphasis became so great that by the late 1960s half of the membership of SLA belonged to the Science/Technology Division, and it was necessary to split that division into about a dozen component parts. To this day, of the SLA Division membership assigned to subject interest rather than type of activity, 48% fall roughly into areas of science and technology.

SPECIAL LIBRARIES SINCE 1970

Continued growth within the special library profession since 1970 cannot be as accurately traced as during the "golden" age of scientific and technical information expansion. Certainly, an emphasis on science and technology, in both the governmental and industrial sectors, continues. However, the period of the 1970s can probably be more accurately described as one of particular growth in special libraries serving commercial and business organizations and in libraries concerned with evolving social and human services.

The Business and Finance Division is now the largest single division of SLA, and the Social Science Division, which includes sections dealing with International Affairs, Urban Affairs and Social Welfare, stands in second place. It would not really be surprising if the 1980s saw a resurgence of special library service in the humanities areas. Certainly, as leisure time grows, more organizations devoted to cultural and recreational activities are likely to emerge.

All special library activity is of course highly influenced by general economic trends and is not immune to recessions or depressions. Special libraries in corporations are funded from gross or operating profits. Where profits are small or nonexistent, libraries are affected, as in the economic downturns of 1975 and 1981. However, by late 1983 special libraries showed a vigorous recovery, reflecting business recovery, while academic and public libraries were still squeezed in financial vises, including taxpayer revolts, the malaise of the educational system and the decline of the inner city.

By and large, American special libraries, tied to the larger private industry economic spectrum, have benefitted more than they have suffered. Faith in the future growth of special libraries in the United States is, to some extent, tied to a faith in the future of the economy and the free enterprise system.

MEDICAL LIBRARIES

No discussion of the development of special libraries can be complete without specific consideration of medical libraries. As already noted, medical libraries were among the first special libraries, and the separation of medical librarians into a distinct professional association preceded that of other special librarians by more than a decade. Indeed, Kathleen Birchette has traced the development of medical libraries from 2000 B.C.

National Priorities and Support

Humanists might disagree with the emphases, but throughout the history of this country, and for that matter most other countries, the support of medical—and also agricultural—research has been given a high priority. It is therefore not surprising that this sense of urgency should extend to library development as well. This point can probably be made most simply by pointing out that the United States has three national libraries, one serving medicine, one serving agriculture and one serving everything that is left over (the Library of Congress). Developing countries in Asia and Africa whose national library development has largely been patterned on that of the United States have tended to follow this example and this set of priorities.

The Medical Library Assistance Act

The support for medical libraries at the national level has been consistently more dramatic and effective than general support for libraries included in such legislation as the Higher Education Act or the Library Services Construction Act, or as subsumed or assumed in revenue sharing legislation, from which libraries receive little if anything. Medical library assistance reached its culmination in the passage of the Medical Library Assistance Act of 1965 (MLAA), a piece of legislation that has since been amended and to some extent curtailed, but also one that has been continued with little political fear of termination. The fight against disease is still a popular rallying point.

MLAA authorized programs in eight areas:

- Construction of facilities

- Training in medical library sciences

- Special scientific projects

- Research and development in medical library science and related fields

- Improvement and expansion of the basic resources of medical libraries

- Establishment of regional medical libraries

- Support of biomedical publication

- Regional branches of the National Library of Medicine

While the last of these areas has never been implemented, the others have had a significant impact on the development of medical librarianship and of medical libraries. They raised the National Library of Medicine (NLM) to a point of eminence where it could accurately be stated in the late 1960s and the 1970s that NLM was in the forefront of library experimentation and development. During this period, in fact, NLM was probably unique in that its authorizing legislation recognized and funded basic as well as applied research programs. Most libraries, including special libraries, find that whatever interest they have in experimentation must be piggybacked on existing operating programs and existing operational funding.

MEDLARS/MEDLINE and the Regional Medical Library Program

Two portions of the assistance act program deserve specific mention, although they will not be discussed in detail, as they are amply described in other literature. The development of the MEDLARS/MEDLINE data base, and access to it, made it possible for medical libraries large and small, and researchers where there were no libraries, to achieve bibliographic access to a very large and intensively analyzed body of literature.

The Regional Medical Library Program (RMLP) was designed to provide wide support for the delivery to libraries of material not in their collection. It did this through the establishment of a network, with the National Library of Medicine as the comprehensive national resource linked to 11 regional medical libraries and through them to smaller libraries, creating a chain for document delivery through interlibrary loan. The entire process was originally subsidized through the National Library of Medicine. The program therefore supported not only bibliographic access to the vast resources of NLM (and, through NLM, of the world) but also research and development to improve bibliographic access as well as document delivery.

This was a crucial step in the development of medical libraries, because it made it possible for any small hospital or research facility to derive tremendous benefits, even through the minimal expenditure for a small collection, one librarian and a computer terminal. While later versions of the program have included modifications to make the program more financially self-sufficient, the initial support funding was essential to put the program in place. Even entrepreneurially oriented special and medical librarians might agree that if the service has now proven worthwhile, it is perhaps time for the benefitting organizations to help pay for it.

The medical library experience establishes a superb model for the encouragement of library service development in other areas, because it recognizes both of the fundamental parts of any successful library cooperative activity—bibliographic access and document delivery. Too many systems have historically delivered the first but only suggested the second, an intolerable situation for special librarians, who are so often under time pressures in their search for information.

SUMMARY

Special libraries, then, have developed in response to both the growing need for information and the growing supply of information in our increasingly technological society. Despite economic setbacks, the number of special libraries has continued to grow steadily in the past 100 years. Businesses in particular have recognized the advantages of improving access to information. In Chapter 3, we will turn from the general to the specific, with a look at the process of actually establishing a special library and at the services and objectives appropriate to it.

SUGGESTED ADDITIONAL READINGS

Adams, Scott. "The National Library of Medicine." Chapter 11 in *The Handbook of Medical Library Practice*, Third Edition, edited by Gertrude L. Annan and Jacqueline W. Felter. Chicago: Medical Library Association, 1970, pp. 331-346.

Birchette, Kathleen P. "The History of Medical Libraries from 2000 B.C. to 1900 A.D." *Bulletin of the Medical Library Association* 61:302-308 (July 1973).

Brodman, Estelle. "The Delivery of Medical Information in the 1970s." *Bulletin of the Medical Library Association* 59:579-584 (October 1971).

Christianson, Elin B. "Special Libraries: Putting Knowledge to Work." *Library Trends* 25:399-416 (July 1976).

Garvey, William D. *Communication, the Essence of Science.* Elmsford, NY: Pergamon Press, Inc., 1979.

Hendricks, Donald B. "The Regional Medical Library Program." *Library Trends* 24:331-345 (October 1975).

Kruzas, Anthony T. *Business and Industrial Libraries in the United States, 1820-1940*. New York: Special Libraries Association, 1965.

Pings, Vern M. "Regional Medical Libraries: A Concept and a Necessity." *Bulletin of the Medical Library Association* 59:242-246 (April 1971).

3

Purposes and Objectives

The preceding chapter discussed at some length the development and establishment of special libraries, but we have given no consideration to how this process actually occurs. In the academic environment the answer is relatively simple. The existence of adequate libraries is tied to the evaluation of the academic program. You cannot have an accredited college or university, or a degree program accepted by professional associations such as the American Chemical Society, without demonstrating that you have library resources which meet the expectations of the reviewers.

Public libraries, although they must meet no formal or legal standard, still fall under the scrutiny of government funding bodies, chambers of commerce or other community groups, who will quickly complain if local library service ranks below that of a rival community. State library agencies also provide some level of standards and control. For special libraries, particularly in the private sector, no such comparisons exist. Stockholders have been known to complain about many things, but never about the quality of the corporate library.

"UNPLANNED" LIBRARIES

To a considerable extent special libraries simply come into being through the accumulation of books, periodicals and other records, which have been bought or donated, or which represent a record of the organization's own research efforts. Inevitably, these files continue to grow. Some of them are strong collections; some of them are simply the refuse that nobody else wants. Eventually, frustration with these files, their inaccessibility, the loss, disappearance and misplacement of material known to be there, all reach the point where the decision is made that "something" must be done. Frequently, that something involves the appointment or hiring of a clerk, and the decision can be a crucial point in the determination of future directions. For this reason, the Special Libraries Association has a program of consultation services, which is initially free, to advise management on its alternatives for future directions.

A particular point must be made here: The managers who must decide what sort of special library to establish don't know what they want, but they usually recognize that they don't know and are willing to have advice. Special librarians are lucky. The users of academic libraries don't know either, but by contrast they think they do.

The development of special libraries, then, comes quite frequently not from a carefully conceived organizational plan, but from a frustration that has finally reached the breaking point. It is not surprising under this continually shifting scenario that nobody really knows how many special libraries there are or when a collection of books, journals and reports becomes a library.

SIGNS THAT A LIBRARY IS NEEDED

Special Libraries: A Guide for Management, Second Edition, lists some specific guideposts or warning signals which suggest to organizational managers that it is time to establish a library.

• The perception that funds are being wasted in the purchase of multiple copies of books and periodicals because of a lack of centralization and control.

• Large and expensive collections of materials scattered in offices or in storerooms, where they take up considerable space and still don't yield the desired item when it is demanded.

• A flood of mail announcing new publications, information services and data bases that nobody has the time or the inclination to screen to determine those of interest.

• An awareness by organizational professionals, from contact with others at professional gatherings, that they are not keeping up with developments in their fields. This is particularly unsettling for researchers, but it is also disturbing for business executives if they suspect that there are things others know and they don't.

The *Guide* also suggests reasons that are more direct and immediate and that might lead to a higher level of initial expectation for library and information service. These include:

• Professionals are spending a great deal of time in the attempt to track down needed information, including trips to other libraries.

• An important decision has to be delayed because the needed information simply has not been found.

• There is evidence of duplicated effort, with a resulting waste of both time and money, because the results of earlier work simply were not known.

ORGANIZATIONAL SUPPORT FOR A LIBRARY

On occasion the decision to consider establishing a library and information center is a conscious and deliberate one and not as the result of the pressure of other factors. This usually occurs because an individual newly brought into the organizational structure at a high level of authority knows from past experience the value of a strong information service and insists that the same level of service is needed here. In this case, much of the need for initial justification can be avoided because the point has already been accepted. Unfortunately, this does not happen too frequently. Most organizations tend to promote from within; thus executives accept the present level of information service because they have known no other.

The importation of new executives can also pose a risk if the organization already has a high level of information service and the new arrival comes from a place where it was poorer or more passive. This may cause a need to rejustify a level of service that had been assumed to be safely established and accepted.

All of the above leads to a central proposition, which will be emphasized throughout this book, because it forms the cornerstone for organizations' reactions to their libraries and information centers: Individuals tend to react on a highly personal basis, by supporting things that please and assist them and by ignoring those things that do not affect their work. Being ignored in organizational dynamics is as bad as being opposed, since those who ignore you support some other unit in its drive for scarce resources that might otherwise go to you.

Individual professionals not only react personally to the concept of the library or information service, they react personally to individual staff members. The closest and surest bond that can be established is that between the library and organizational professionals who have found one staff member whom they trust to understand specific needs and help solve specific problems. The fact that this selected reference source happens to be your cataloger is irrelevant to them and, if ultimately necessary, must be irrelevant to you. Edward Strable, manager of the J. Walter Thompson Co. Information Center, reports that retired Thompson executives still make use of this resource for their information needs. As Strable has pointed out: "You never lose a satisfied customer."

THE PURPOSE OF A SPECIAL LIBRARY

Assuming then that a special library has been or is about to be established, what is it supposed to do? Here the motto of the Special Libraries Association—"Putting Knowledge to Work"—provides a useful guideline. *The special library exists to support and enhance the mission of the organization in which it is housed.* It has no purpose beyond this, and in this very pragmatic evaluation tool can be seen what is undoubtedly the most significant difference between special and other kinds of libraries. The wise special librarian never loses sight of this distinction, even if his or her managers occasionally do. During periods of financial stress the question will arise even if it has been dormant for years, and, as James M. Matarazzo has shown, the results can be disastrous.

Identifying the Mission of the Organization

What is the mission of the organization which is to house the library? Surprisingly, although it is presumably known by organizational management, it is rarely articulated and almost never discussed within the context of library planning. On a number of occasions this writer has served as a consultant to corporate management in the planning process for the establishment of a special library. Corporate contacts invariably try to bring the discussion immediately to levels of detail—how large a staff, how much space, how many books and subscriptions, how large a budget?

They are surprised to be told that before those questions can be answered, this consultant has a few of his own:

• What do you do at present and what do you hope to do five and ten years from now?

• What products do you presently manufacture and what concerns do you have about your continuing share of the marketplace?

• Without divulging sensitive information, in what areas of research are you particularly interested?

• What sort of information problems are you having? What sort of frustrations and time delays are you encountering?

• Is your organization growing—in number of people, in number of locations, in diversity of products and services?

• What is being done now when information is needed, because even in the absence of any library service something happens?

The barrage of questions sometimes causes surprises, but it usually brings answers. Although users and managers don't always automatically make the connection, they will agree if pushed that a level of library and information service can only be defined in terms of organizational needs, and on no other basis. This writer, again while serving as a consultant, concluded one evaluation report by stating that the organization had defined the level of information service by the "need" to spend $150,000 on the library, no more and no less. The point was effectively received; the listeners recognized both its truth and its absurdity.

The For-profit Sector

What then is the organizational mission—or, more frequently, are the organizational missions—that the library or information center must support if it is to have any validity at all? It is not always as easy to answer the question as might be supposed. For those special libraries that exist in the for-profit center, the question has at least one immediate and simple answer. In these organizations there is an overriding requirement that a profit be made, if not in any one specific year then at least over a range of years. In a profit-centered environment, ultimately nothing else matters. A product of superior design that cannot be sold with a profitable price markup counts for little.

Here again are the seeds of a lesson for special librarians, which will have further discussion later. In the commercial sector in particular, although in other sectors as well, it is how well the organization as a whole performs, and not just the performance of individual units, that affects support for the library. This is a lesson that libraries which emphasize service to research and development groups especially need to remember. If one group were served at 100% effectiveness and three others not at all, an overall rating of 25% is not unreasonable, and that is a failing grade.

The Not-for-profit Sector

Libraries outside the for-profit sector have overall organizational goals to identify which are not quite as easy to spotlight. And yet the process of identifying overall mission is the same. The director of a historical museum and his or her governing board have clearly identified some overall directions for the institution. These may involve questions of financial strengthening by attracting and retaining sponsors and individual members. Does the library have a role to play in this process by issuing publications supplied to benefactors, by providing reference services or simply by maintaining an attractive and professional environment to which potential contributors will react positively?

Program managers in governmental organizations have very clear goals and objectives, and tying the library's activities to these is just as appropriate as in the private industrial sector. Professional societies also have their objectives, which may range from a drive to increase members to an improvement in membership services to justify the most recent dues increase. Are reference services or information among those services? Are they potential services?

SERVING ORGANIZATIONAL GOALS

Whatever the organizational setting in which the special library is housed, there are overall organizational goals that will ultimately determine where funds are allocated. It is essential for the special librarian to determine what these goals are and to develop plans for supporting them. The managers who decide to establish a special library usually have rather limited hopes and expectations. They want someone to maintain order for the collection already established and to purchase and arrange additional materials as requested. They will be satisfied with any librarian who does this and nothing else. Competent special librarians know, however, that this level of service does not represent a good special library and that much, much more can be accomplished to serve the needs of the organization. Providing a higher level of service may become a very real issue when competitive budgetary decisions are made. Special librarians who become so engrossed in the operational details of daily activities that they lose sight of their larger purpose run a grave risk.

Fundamentally, organizations establish, support, continue and enlarge their special libraries for only one reason—because the organization is better served in its overall objectives by having a library than by not having one. In making that determination, management operates largely by observation and instinct, and by the specific reaction of users and non-users. It is really not whether or not the organization is better served, but whether it believes it is.

In the for-profit organization, for which such comparisons are much easier to make, the library, like every other organizational unit, is supposed to make its contribution to corporate success and profitability. However, that connection is not easily made. Individuals responsible within a manufacturing organization for production costs or for sales dollars can be, and usually are, held directly accountable and are rewarded or punished accordingly. The contribution of the special library is by no means as clear or as measurable, and there are several reasons for this.

First, the library does not have a monopoly on the provision of information services, although its managers would be well advised to make its users as dependent on the library as possible. However successful this effort, professionals in the organization still have other forms of access to information—by talking to colleagues, by attending professional meetings and in some cases by making their own arrangements to secure publications or to access data bases.

Second, the library's activities lack the "proof" that, in scientific experimentations, is provided through a control group. If it is the special library manager's premise that access to a strong and active information collection makes the organization and its employees more effective, then any proof for that assertion ultimately would have to come from the identification of a body of users who are denied service, and who can be shown to have failed. This is the way in which the effect of a vitamin deficiency is demonstrated with laboratory animals. Of course, it cannot be done with professionals in the organizational setting.

Finally, efficiencies and cost reductions achieved through library services are not recoverable as lessened expenditures among user groups, and accountants know this. A technical program manager may be enthusiastic about the quality of library support, but his enthusiasm will stop well short of volunteering to reduce his own organizational staff in exchange for good library service. Recruitment brochures for the special library profession occasionally highlight specific cost reductions achieved by the library's ability to pinpoint and avoid the duplication of a research effort. Such accomplishments can be real enough, but they form a tenuous basis for continued support of library activities, because they can rarely be repeated at regular intervals.

Fortunately for librarians, such specific justifications of direct contribution to profit are not normally expected as tangible forms of proof. What is expected, and must be delivered, is the appearance of a contribution to overall organizational programs. That appearance comes most significantly from the testimony and support of professional users, preferably a broad cross-section of them.

SERVING RESEARCH AND DEVELOPMENT NEEDS

The activities of most special libraries, like the activities of academic libraries, are directly in support of organizational research and development functions and tend to ignore other activities. There are several very obvious reasons for this. Researchers depend on two sources of substantiation, laboratory investigation and the literature. While for some types of work there is no substitute for the former, even it can be speeded and simplified by library use. It is both faster and cheaper to find the results of an experiment in the literature rather than in the laboratory. In other fields, such as economics research, experiments are not really practical, while in such areas as marketing research the final test design might be heavily based on a literature review.

Researchers, unlike many other special library users, are heavily dependent on literature and other information sources. They also tend to come to the library as "trained" library users, frequently directly from academic posts or the completion of advanced degrees. Having an experienced and knowledgeable user can present problems as well as advantages. The expectation these individuals bring is usually for the kind of passive self-service relationship that they have come to know in the educational environment. It is difficult for some organizational researchers not only to make the transition from the general search for knowledge to research for an end objective, but also to increase their expectations for interactive service to a level more in keeping with the organization's clear need to make tangible, rapid progress.

SERVING OTHER CLIENTELE

Regardless of how well or badly special libraries serve researchers, they invariably find this group as their most clearly identifiable service clientele. Many—perhaps a majority—of special libraries are initially developed by the research organization to serve the research organization. Service to other professionals within the organization is frequently much more haphazard, and sometimes nonexistent. It is important to broaden the library's clientele to include others besides researchers, in large part because it is these other individuals who ultimately have the power to determine expenditure levels and priorities.

Unfortunately, these people are not always easily served. Sometimes this is in part because researchers jealously guard both library collections and the time of librarians to retain their own priorities. It is in part also because these other potential users have needs that do not easily fit the "unplanned" special library, which usually develops along academic library traditions—large collections developed for individuals who like to browse, who already know what they want or who know how to use the research tools of their own fields. Other users—from corporate administration, from production, from advertising and sales, from accounting and from personnel administration—need information that differs from what is frequently found in the collection. They also have different information gathering habits and different end uses.

Herbert Brinberg, president of Aspen Systems Corp. of Rockville, MD, speaking at the 1980 Congress of the International Federation for Documentation in Copenhagen, defined three groups of users by their information needs and habits. Researchers, he suggested, seek raw library materials that they can then sift and analyze. Engineers, sales personnel and production managers largely seek specific answers to specific questions. They usually need these immediately because of a failure to plan ahead adequately. They frequently don't have any idea of where to look and don't really want to take the time. They would prefer simply to turn over the problem to someone who will supply the answer in a short time. They tend not to come to the library at all because they have little experience or expectation of success in such transactions and because they feel that the library will not allow them to interact on their terms. It is largely these individuals who, in keeping with the predictions of Calvin Mooers, will make assumptions and guesses rather than look for answers, because looking for answers is too much trouble.

The third group identified by Brinberg includes managers who are looking neither for raw informational materials nor specific answers but rather for viable alternatives with regard to what decisions are possible. Brinberg argues that libraries, including special libraries, largely fail to attract and serve a wide body of users because they are constructed and oriented specifically to the service only of researchers. The danger in organizational dynamics and organizational politics of such narrowly defined service is a recurrent theme in this book.

TYPES OF SERVICE PROVIDED

In addition to a categorization by service clientele, the purposes and objectives of special libraries can also be grouped by the types of services provided and needs met.

Support of Recognized Information Needs

Support of recognized information needs, usually expressed as document requests, represents the main purpose, and in some instances the entire responsibility, of the special library organization. Quite simply, this level of service hinges on determining what the professionals in the organization are doing and what information support is needed to do it.

Several pitfalls to accomplishing this have already been identified. Perhaps the most likely is that organizational needs are frequently narrowly defined to be the needs of one specialized constituency, usually researchers. Other needs are not served, in part because that service is discouraged by those who control the library, and in part because other professionals don't volunteer what they are doing and what they need. The maintenance of communications channels to learn what is happening and what the problems are is one of the most important tasks of the special library manager. In fact, it may be his or her most significant task. It should not be assumed that libraries in a research organization will necessarily be told what research projects are under way, planned or contemplated.

The level of service in response to recognized organizational information needs can be either reactive or proactive and anticipatory. The quality of reactive service hinges in large part on the adequacy of the in-house collection and on the ability to obtain information from other libraries. This ability, in turn, is greatly dependent on the adequacy of clerical staffing to submit the orders, a continuing and nagging problem in almost all special libraries and one that deserves special attention.

Much better than reactive service, of course, is proactive or anticipatory service. From an organizational standpoint this has two benefits. First, it provides useful information more rapidly than if it had to be requested. Second, it provides information that might otherwise not be requested at all. For the special library manager, the development of a proactive and anticipatory service provides the best and perhaps the only opportunity to interact with the user at a level which he or she will recognize as a professional interaction. It may be uncharitable, and it is certainly controversial, but professional users tend to look at the reactive provision of requested specific books and periodicals as a clerical or at best an administrative function, whether it is performed well or not.

One final caution. The provision of anticipatory and proactive information is not a numbers game, with the winner delivering the largest stack of paper. Many librarians tend to measure quality as though it were quantity (size of collection, size of circulation). Library users, and even more the nonusers frequently represented in such groups as management and marketing, are extremely nervous about the threat of delivery of more information from the library when they haven't yet read what was delivered last month. Given the value system employed by these individuals, circulation statistics might be considered an *inverse* measurement of the quality of an information service: the less exact the service, the more it must supply.

Support of Educational and Training Programs

For some organizations the commitment to education and training is heavy; sometimes it is embedded in union contracts and other employee agreements. For the library to take on this responsibility not only provides a meaningful and needed service but also broadens the user base and provides a potential security net for times of organization stress and crisis. Cutting the library is not as easy if a contractual activity may be affected.

A Public Relations and Public Image Tool

Obviously, the public relations role is more significant in a major corporate headquarters location than in a field laboratory in the middle of the Dakota Black Hills. It also suits the needs of some organizations—those that encourage public awareness—more than it does others. The development of an attractive as well as a functionally useful library is particularly important in some not-for-profit settings such as art museums, historical societies and professional associations with broad membership. It is also potentially important for corporations that are concerned about public image and public perception, such as public utility companies. Public image is obviously less significant or totally insignificant for organizations where access is restricted or forbidden because of considerations of security or sensitivity of information. It is nevertheless an opportunity that, if presented, should not be ignored.

The library still represents for any organization a potentially attractive area to show visitors, yet at the same time it gives less of an appearance of "frill" to stockholders than a clubhouse or swimming pool. In designing such a library, functional efficiency and attractive appearance are not mutually exclusive considerations, although it is sometimes necessary to be both patient and firm with the architects involved in the process, who may forget their own professional teaching that form should follow function.

Records Management and Archival Functions

Combining a library with records and archival management is a fairly recent development in organizational structure, but also one which makes a great deal of sense. Executives have become increasingly aware of the importance of maintaining complete, accurate and retrievable records of past performance. Part of this is because of a growing awareness of history and the recognition that much can be learned from the past. A probably greater reason lies in legal requirements, in terms of both government regulations and the threat of litigation. Most organizations, particularly in the corporate sector, have not developed an expertise for dealing with these problems and these concerns, except perhaps in very large companies.

Combining these functions with the library or information center is logical, and combining them under the management and authority of the library manager is certainly more attractive to our profession than combining them under the authority of the records manager. The concepts of file development and retrieval that form the basis of librarianship are very similar to those used in records systems and, for that matter, in inventory records, banks and insurance companies. Subsuming a corporate records center or archive under the management structure already in place for the special library or information center provides a particular opportunity for broadened visibility and access throughout the organization, because the records management and archival functions generally provide contact with individuals who are not necessarily heavy library users. It must, of course, be stressed that with additional responsibilities additional resources and personnel must also be provided.

General Information and Recreational Reading

Unless it is included as a specific charge from the highest levels of organizational management, special libraries should avoid designing their collections for general and recreational use. Most users of special libraries have the same access as other citizens to public libraries. Many are also users of academic libraries, and their children have the use of school libraries for their own work. There are situations in which the special library may provide the only available library service and therefore must serve as a general or public library. A hospital library serving both medical staff and patients is one such obvious example; a library serving an oil drilling operation on the North Slope of Alaska is a less obvious but nevertheless just as real instance. But such situations are relatively rare.

Mixing of functions should be avoided where possible, not only because it dilutes both the focus and resources of the library and information service, but also because it lends fuel to the inevitable suspicion of some managers that time spent in the library is time spent away from productive work. That generalization is probably specious and will not normally arouse much upper level management support. (The library manager must also resist any suggestion that he or she check on individuals using the library to see what they are doing; if such scrutiny is desirable at all, it is their manager's own responsibility.) It is not only inappropriate but also impolitic to provide the library collection with copies of daily newspapers and of general magazines, unless the library is one in which such access is important, as might be the case in a newspaper or advertising library. It would be less likely in a high technology engineering firm.

As stated at the outset of this chapter, it is important for the special librarian to take an inventory of the purposes and objectives and, from these the programs, of the organization being served, in order to develop the list of activities that should be undertaken to support the organizational mission. It is equally important to determine what should *not* be undertaken, because inappropriate service misdirects attention and resources from activities of greater importance.

A POLITICAL CAUTION

The reader will certainly have noticed the emphasis in this book on organizational planning and political strategy. This is not only inevitable; it is essential. Special librarians and information managers must be intelligent, and they must be well educated in the areas important and common to all kinds of librarians. Special subject training may also be necessary. However, there is still more.

The operation of special libraries (in truth, the operation of all libraries) takes place in a highly political and competitive environment. It is one of the characteristics of organizational dynamics that resources rarely if ever approach the level of demand for them. The competition for funds is therefore an ongoing political process, an exercise for which many librarians are ill prepared both in their academic coursework and in their personal value system. The political process is sometimes ugly, but more often it takes place within ground rules as formalized as those of an athletic contest. If librarians are to retain their share, or perhaps to do a little better than that, they must understand the dynamics of the organization in which their competition for funds takes place, whether the arena is an academic institution, a municipal administration, a government agency, a foundation or a corporation.

All libraries are ultimately judged, and rewarded or punished, through the awarding or withholding of resources by nonlibrarians, who do not necessarily share the concerns or understand the standards of librarians. Special librarians probably have an advantage over their colleagues in other libraries because of their earlier recognition that the value of the library will ultimately be judged by what it does or does not do to support the mission and objectives of the larger organization.

SUGGESTED ADDITIONAL READINGS

Drucker, Peter F. Op. cit.

Kok, John. "Now That I'm in Charge, What Do I Do?" *Special Libraries* 71:523-528 (December 1980).

Lechner, Marian G. "Organization of a Recreational Library." In *Readings in Special Librarianship*, edited by Harold S. Sharp. New York: Scarecrow Press, Inc., 1963, pp. 114-121.

Special Libraries: A Guide for Management, Second Edition. Op. cit.

White, Herbert S. "Organizational Placement of the Special Library, Its Relationship to Success and Survival." *Special Libraries* 64:141-144 (March 1973).

4

Standards, Professionalism and Salaries

Professional associations usually take a very active role in both the development and enforcement of standards in their areas of expertise. The most visible examples are in professional accreditation controls applied at the state level by associations of doctors, dentists and lawyers. Completion of a degree does not qualify an individual to become a doctor, dentist or lawyer; it is also necessary to pass an examination administered by those already in the field, and a considerable number of aspiring professionals fail the examination.

A number of reasons are ascribed to a profession's desire to control its standards and to monitor the quality of those who elect to join its ranks. Critics might argue that it is an easy way to restrict entry, limit competition, and insure scarcity and high salaries. Some of these complaints might have a share of validity, but there are still good reasons for professional monitoring, and it is generally agreed that professionals are best qualified to evaluate their colleagues. Gresham's Law of Economics, which states that bad money will drive good money from the marketplace, is also appropriate in other disciplines. The acceptance of lower standards for educational qualifications or performance on the job invariably has a depressing effect on an overall profession, because unqualified or less qualified candidates almost always turn out to be cheaper.

DIFFICULTIES OF ESTABLISHING PROFESSIONAL STANDARDS

The library profession has never been successful in promulgating and enforcing professional standards to the extent to which our colleagues in law and medicine have been able to control licensing and access.

Use—and Misuse—of the Title "Librarian"

Anyone attending concerts will see listed among the musicians, usually after the percussion section or harpists, one or more individuals identified as "librarians." The duties performed by these individuals include primarily the appropriate marking of scores and their placement on the correct stands but never the determination of what composer's music to distribute or to whom to give the first violinist's part. As large centralized computer facilities evolved in the 1960s, they brought with them the job title of Tape Librarian, whose clerical task it was to log tapes in and out of a central repository. Only the switch from tapes to disks, and not any perception of the inappropriateness of the title, may now bring about a change in the nomenclature. Finally, we all know of volunteers or clerks who stamp due dates into the backs of books and yet call themselves librarians. It is a recognized problem for the profession that indeed some members of the general public refer to these individuals as librarians.

Educational Standards

Librarians have battled on occasion for the status that control over qualifications carries, with at best mixed success, and sometimes even over the heated objection of other librarians who consider arbitrarily stated educational qualifications as overly restrictive. Librarianship is one of the few professions with such guilt pangs. The tug-of-war with the education profession over the qualification of school librarians was largely lost a long time ago. School librarians must qualify as fully accepted teachers. The additional library skills required to be allowed to perform in a library are far less strictly stated.

Graduation from a library education program accredited by the American Library Association is still considered an absolute requirement for a number of academic and major public libraries, but these requirements are increasingly under legal attack as well as pressure from government agencies. ALA has, perhaps surprisingly, made no real efforts to protect and defend the importance of its own accreditation process.

None of the foregoing should be interpreted as a blanket endorsement of the kind of rigid control practiced by lawyers and doctors, because there are invariably excesses in any such process. However, it is equally demonstrable that in the absence of yardsticks with legal or at least moral support, employers and other managers find the taking of economic shortcuts very tempting.

Accreditation of Parent Organizations

Libraries in universities accredited by regional bodies, or medical or legal libraries that fall under the control of these professions, are covered to a considerable extent by accreditation procedures and standards already developed for these fields, which secondarily affect libraries as part of the evaluation process. For example, the *Accreditation Manual for Hospitals* developed in 1978 by the Joint Commission on the Accreditation of Hospitals states in part: "The hospital shall provide library services to meet the informational, educational and, when appropriate, the research-related needs of the medical and hospital staffs." This general statement is then amplified and clarified: "The professional library services shall be organized to assure appropriate direction of supervision, staffing and resources," and "The provision of professional library service shall be guided by written policies and procedures."

Helpful and supportive as these statements are, they are silent as to the specific status and qualifications of the "professionals" so designated; it is possible that they might mean health sciences professionals as an acceptable replacement for library professionals. Accreditation standards developed for other library specializations concentrate on the size and arrangement of the library space provided, on the number of volumes in the collection and on the adequacy of student seating.

ALA Standards for Libraries

To a large degree, standards for public, academic and school libraries promulgated by ALA carry forward this presumed equation of size of collection with indication of quality. Standards speak to numbers of volumes required to serve adequately various sizes of public and student populations. It should already be clear that such numerical criteria would by themselves have little value for special libraries with their small and specialized collections, which might be, perhaps ought to be, actively weeded (numerical standards would seem to imply that weeding of obsolete material worsens collections!), and with a management little impressed either with numerical competition or the potential threat of sanctions applied in academia.

Professional Society Standards

Library professional societies are also at best ambivalent with regard to the enforcement of standards for either initial or continued education. As already noted, ALA has the responsibility for the accreditation of qualified educational programs of the masters level but leaves to individual libraries the question of whether to insist on graduates from such sanctioned programs. Certainly membership in ALA is not conditioned on any sort of educational level, proficiency test or evidence of continuing education.

The Special Libraries Association, while it occasionally hears member complaints that its viewpoints are not adequately represented in the accreditation process, has yet to focus on a specific list of things it would like to include in the process. Given the diversity of its membership interests, it is probably not likely to be able to do so. After heated discussion in the late 1960s, SLA voted to remove a formal degree requirement for full membership and to require instead a bachelor's degree plus three years of professional experience, or seven years of professional experience for individuals who could presumably be high school or grade school graduates. The determination of an applicant's professional status is assigned to a committee, but this group can only evaluate the professionalism of the duties assigned, not the professional performance of those duties. Associate membership, which qualifies the applicant for all of the privileges of full membership except the dubious honor of being allowed to hold association-wide office, is open to any applicant who has a serious interest in the objectives of the Association, and presumably that qualification is met through the submittal of a dues check.

The writer recognizes that the above statement may appear as critical or even as sarcastic, but that is not really the intent. There is no particular evidence that unqualified people are storming the gates. Rather, the point is that librarians, including special librarians, are unwilling and probably unable to enforce qualifications for accepted professional status. SLA, probably to a greater extent than other bodies, has provided facilitative mechanisms for continuing education but has not considered relating completion of continuing education units to degrees of status within the association, let alone attempting to convince employers of what action they should or should not take.

MEDICAL LIBRARY ASSOCIATION STANDARDS

This situation can be contrasted to the general policies that education societies and unions have designed for school systems, which require continued courses and degrees for salary increases, promotions and in some cases even retention of the post being held. Only the Medical Library Association, perhaps emboldened by the example of professional requirements in medical practice, has attempted to develop individual qualification requirements with enforcement provisions. In 1978 MLA developed a certification program for medical librarians, which is based not only on graduation from library school and completion of an approved course in medical librarianship but also on a passing grade on an examination administered by MLA plus two years of postgraduate experience.

Even more significantly, certification is not the lifetime "union card" normally represented by library degrees but must be revalidated every five years through continuing education activities and individual accomplishments. Since the recertification process is still in its very early stages, it is not yet possible to determine either the impact of the program on individual activity or the incentive or control that it provides for those who hire or promote medical librarians. In the long run, however, it is how employers view these requirements, and not how librarians look at them, that will decide their effectiveness.

OBJECTIVES AND STANDARDS FOR SPECIAL LIBRARIES

A problem with standards for special librarians can already be seen to emerge. The reluctance to adopt minimum standards of collection size promulgated by other parts of the library profession is understandable, since special libraries serve very diverse goals, depending on their parent organizations. As Logan Cowgill and Robert Havlik have pointed out, special libraries lack accurate historical data as well as quantitative data describing present-day special libraries. We don't even know how many special libraries there are, only how many have representation in professional associations or allow themselves to be listed in the *American Library Directory*. In addition, the development of standards is hampered by an absence of generally accepted definitions for describing the special library universe, by a total diversity of collections, content, size, procedures, facilities and staff, and finally by a lack of consistency in the responsibilities assigned by nonlibrary management.

There is yet another, frequently unspoken, reluctance to adopt standards. Standards are intended as minimums, but the pressure is usually to meet them and not to surpass them. Unless the standards are so idealistic as to be almost meaningless, they are quickly perceived as a threat by those library managers who have succeeded in building organizations that exceed the quantified standards expressed. Special librarians, as entrepreneurs, have an aversion to minimum standards that become defacto maximum standards. Salary data, probably the most sensitive of all informational criteria, are carefully collected but are no longer published in a broad release but appear now as a separate pamphlet, *SLA Triennial Salary Survey*. It is assumed that the special librarian will either use comparable salary data to his or her advantage or make sure that higher management never gets to see this information at all.

Given this level of conflicting interests, it is not surprising that SLA struggled for many years in the vain attempt to develop any sort of standards that could be accepted by its membership. That it was ultimately able to do so is a tribute to a committee under the direction of Samuel Sass and Agnes Brite and especially to committee member Ruth Leonard, a faculty member at the Simmons College Graduate Library School and the recipient in 1965 of the Association's greatest honor, its Professional Award.

Published in the December 1964 issue of *Special Libraries* under the title "Objectives and Standards for Special Libraries," these standards have stood the test of almost 20 years, precisely because they avoid the inclusion of quantitative criteria, which are not only frequently inappropriate but which also rapidly become obsolete. There is no suggestion of numbers of books and periodicals, of expected circulation or of staff size. There is only the much more useful indication of criteria to be met and accomplishments to be achieved. When the document was reissued by SLA in 1970 as a separate pamphlet, its title was shortened to *Objectives for Special Libraries*, and the initially appended standard specifications were dropped, but otherwise it was unchanged.

The following consideration of special library standards uses these standards as a framework for discussion, in recognition of both their logical arrangement and their lasting value. Direct quotes are indicated by quotation marks.

A MAJOR SOURCE OF INFORMATION

"The special library is a major source of information in the organization it serves." The statement could not very well claim that libraries should be *the* major source of information without defining areas of responsibility more specifically than would be possible for such a general document. What is important is that in those areas in which the special library's charter lies, its activities should be paramount. It becomes a real problem for special librarians to find that they may be unable to perform services because of budgetary limitations, while others are able to do so. If the library can't afford to purchase a book or subscribe to a data base but individual users can, that is a clear indication of difficulty. Politically astute managers understand that power comes in large part not only from what you can do but from what you *exclusively* are able to do. To make the point most directly: If it is indeed true that there aren't enough funds for the library to be able to do something that clearly falls within its sphere of responsibility, then there presumably aren't enough funds for anyone else to do it either.

RELEVANT MATERIALS

"The special library acquires, organizes, maintains, utilizes and disseminates informational materials germane to the organization's activities." This is a well written and encompassing statement. The reader will note that it does not attempt to define the format of information materials or to restrict the content to books and periodicals, as of course it should not.

SERVICE TO ALL WHO HAVE APPROPRIATE NEED

"The special library serves all who have appropriate need of its services." The word "appropriate" is presumably intended to recognize that many such libraries deal with proprietary or security access restrictions and might not be available to outsiders, but the phrase "all who have need" is significant. A corporate research library should serve marketing if its collection contains the necessary information or, even more significantly, if there is no marketing library.

RESPONSIBILITY AND AUTHORITY OF THE ADMINISTRATOR

"The special library administrator is responsible for all administrative and professional functions of the library." It is one of the classic tenets of management theory that responsibility must also carry the necessary authority. For the special library manager this must include ultimate decision-making power in the selection of staff and the development of policies and procedures to make the library or information center work properly.

PROFESSIONAL STAFF

"The special library administrator should be a professional librarian...[and] may delegate to staff librarians administrative and supervisory duties and professional responsibilities....Staff librarians should be professional librarians....Specialists other than librarians may be part of the professional library staff."

These issues are extremely important. Organizations involved in a high degree of subject specialization often feel strongly that candidates for professional library positions must also have subject expertise, frequently as represented by advanced degrees. There are at least two reasons for this insistence. One stems from the genuine belief that subject literature and subject terminology are too complex to permit successful interaction without earlier exposure. The other concerns the fear that professional users will not trust or be willing to work with anyone whom they do not respect as a professional colleague. This is of course related to a failure to accept librarianship as a professional expertise in its own right.

The desire to have both library and subject expertise represented in the professional staff certainly has some validity. All other things being equal, it is undoubtedly preferable to have in a chemical library an individual who is both a competent librarian and a competent chemist. Even in this context, however, the requirement is probably overstated, because of the increasingly interdisciplinary nature of special library collections and the growing specialization of academic preparation. A librarian also educated as an organic chemist is undoubtedly more useful in a library dealing with the literature of organic chemistry but is probably no more prepared to deal with telecommunications or aerospace materials than an intelligent and well-prepared political science or education major.

Most frequently, it is scientific libraries that seek the increasingly scarce specialists, while libraries in other fields such as advertising tend to seek broad and versatile generalists. The problem in technical libraries comes when personnel administrators are unable to find individuals who have both science and library educations. Here the decision is frequently—and, by this standard, wrongly—made to use a technical specialist and teach this individual about librarianship, rather than to hire a librarian who can then learn terminology together with an understanding of specific organizational problems. In large and complex libraries and information centers, there are also jobs for subject-trained specialists, which do not require extensive understanding of the management of information operations. These tasks can include literature searching, translation, indexing and abstracting, and the development of computer systems, for which library education may not be needed. The essential point is that these individuals work under the direction of the library manager, not the reverse.

CONTINUING EDUCATION

"Professional staff members have a continuing responsibility in furthering their education....It is important that [they] participate in professional societies concerned with their specialities." This statement says no more than is already assumed for all other professionals who work in the same organization in which the library or information center is located. The fact that the point must be made at all is a clear recognition that the professional status of librarians is not always automatically accepted, perhaps in part because the title has been usurped by others, perhaps unfortunately in part because not all librarians live up to high standards (although it is hard to believe that all chemists, journalists or economists do either).

In any case, professional activity is a necessity for anyone who is indeed a professional, and employers both know and expect this. It is disturbing to recognize that public librarians are frequently denied the funds and time for professional activity and continuing education when many members of public library boards are doctors and lawyers who certainly understand this need in their own professions. For special librarians the situation is not at all clear. The higher management that controls special libraries has no models and guidelines to follow and in the absence of contrary evidence will do what is cheapest. For these reasons, the standard is important.

NONPROFESSIONAL STAFF

"Nonprofessional staff are responsible for the clerical tasks that support the professional staff's work." Clerical support should be provided in a mix appropriate to the kinds and quantities of services provided. However, in most group dynamics, particularly in organizations that house special libraries and most particularly in the for-profit sector, there is a tendency to minimize clerical staffing. It is sometimes even more difficult to get clerical support than professional support. Almost all organizations live with this phenomenon and attempt to develop strategies for dealing with it.

It is, however, a particularly serious problem for librarians. Libraries depend on clerical routine, and clerical tasks normally take precedence over professional duties. In the absence of adequate clerical support staff, professionals must do the work of clerks. The implications can be clearly seen, and no more probably needs to be stated about the impact of this on both level of service and the perception of status.

ADEQUACY OF THE COLLECTION

The standards stress that the collection must be adequate to the needs of users and the objectives of the organization, and that acquisitions policies must be established. Implied, though not explicitly stated, is what is certainly this writer's assumption: that acquisitions decisions must be made by the library or information center staff, although acquisition recommendations and evaluations are always welcome and should be encouraged. It is also important that the library or information center be kept informed about activities and future plans, so that information needs can be anticipated and not just fulfilled. This chapter will not examine the collection standards in any detail; the SLA publication itself should be read for more information.

SERVICES

The standards for services highlight the rapid delivery of requested items, involvement in interlibrary loan (except for restricted items), the effective dissemination of contents of periodicals, undertaking of literature searches, and compilation of bibliographies and indexes.

These standards also stress the library's provision of translation services, one of the few areas of activity which has probably declined to some degree over the last two decades. A great deal of the literature that originates in other countries is now either published in English or furnished with English language abstracts or summaries. The full translation of articles is in any case an expensive and time-consuming activity. In many cases, the responsible and responsive library manager can control time and cost factors by providing for a translation of the abstract or summary, or by arranging for an individual, whether on the library staff or elsewhere in the organization, who knows the language to meet informally with the requestor. However, the sharing of translations was one of the earliest and most effective areas of special library cooperation.

The section on services standards is conservative and can perhaps be faulted for a lack of foresight. On the other hand, many of the computerized techniques involved in aggressive anticipatory information services were still in their infancy in 1964, and it would probably be unfair to expect the authors to have foreseen what would be possible in the 1980s.

PHYSICAL FACILITIES

The standards for physical facilities stress the needs both for convenient access and for long-term planning. Special libraries should be conveniently accessible to their users, preferably near a place users frequent in any case. Proximity to the cafeteria or the main building entrance become obvious location choices. If the library's location is not convenient, the result may be either the fragmentation or the redundant duplication of the collection. Even worse, the spectre of the ever-present Mooers' Law raises its head. If libraries and information centers are difficult to use, individuals may pretend they didn't need the information in the first place.

Electronic delivery mechanisms, which could not be foreseen in 1964, alleviate this problem considerably, particularly for library users in different buildings or even different cities. Bibliographic access to the collection can be provided through terminals, and the rapid delivery of documents by messenger or through electronic mail is well within our grasp if we are willing to pay for it.

Libraries grow, even with intensive programs for microforming and weeding. In addition, they are not easy to expand or to move. As previously noted, special libraries do not have specifically designated buildings but are forced to compete for space in general office or laboratory areas. It is therefore prudent not only to plan a space allocation that will be adequate for the staff and collection anticipated several years in the future but also to locate the library in an area with no overriding restraints on expansion. Internal partitions separating the library from its neighbors can be moved if the neighbors are relocated, but corridors and the exterior walls of the building resist manipulation. Windows may be nice, but they also preclude further movement in that direction.

BUDGETS

The standard on budgets makes several very telling points. It argues that the initial budget be established in response to the recommendation of the library administrator and that the same administrator have responsibility for both the justification and the expenditure of the budgeted funds. Those statements may seem simplistic and obvious, but they are fraught with significance. Many librarians do indeed have difficulty in making budgetary recommendations based on needs rather than on some administrator's preconceptions. The role of the budgeting process in causing these problems will be discussed in Chapter 8.

The standards also stress that the greater proportion of the library budget be allocated to professional and nonprofessional salaries. This condition does occur in virtually all libraries, and studies have shown that between 60% and 80% of the special library budget is spent on salaries. Why then is the injunction important? The writers of the standards could not have anticipated the rapid growth of the published literature, the increase in prices, which has far outstripped the inflation rate, and the budget cutbacks that occasionally affect all libraries. (Or perhaps they could have, because these are not really new problems but largely restatements of old issues that defy easy solution.)

This standards statement is important because in the traditional self-service library, so prevalent in academia and still the preference or expectation of some special library users, the integrity of the collection is of paramount importance—periodical subscriptions must be renewed and desired books must be purchased. During part of the 1970s, when growth of the professional literature and normal publishing inflation were further compounded by a decline in the foreign purchasing power of the United States dollar, maintaining equivalent collections in academic and some special libraries would have required an annual materials budget growth of about 20%. In the absence of such largesse, user thoughts turn quite naturally to tapping the larger reservoir of funds set aside for personnel staffing and salaries. After all, such users might argue, the focus of a self-service library is on the collection, and if necessary staff can be cut. This is a disastrous strategy for libraries—once the process begins, it has no logical end. It is particularly improper as an approach for special libraries because, as the reader surely already knows, special libraries are judged (or at least should be judged), not by the size of their collections, but by the use made of them. Even reactive use—but certainly all proactive and anticipatory service—requires the existence of a competent library staff.

THE IMPORTANCE OF STANDARDS

The standards developed by Sass, Brite and Leonard 20 years ago are still extremely useful today, and the special library profession is indebted to their pioneering work. This author regrets only that the Special Libraries Association has seen fit to rename the 1964 standards with the much softer and more idealistic term "objectives," to sidetrack them into a special publication rather than periodically display them in directories and handbooks, and to make no real attempt to emphasize that their implementation is important. A profession whose work is so diversified and so little understood must occasionally set aside its affinity for independence and concentrate on searching for those common elements that form the basis for the expression of a professional stance. The Medical Library Association's efforts to put teeth into both education and continuing education through its certification process is a worthy example of such an endeavor, though it is too early to determine whether or not it will succeed.

SALARIES, BENEFITS AND WORKING CONDITIONS

The remainder of this chapter will briefly discuss salaries, fringe benefits and working conditions. As already noted, the Special Libraries Association carefully compiles data on professional salaries but then just as carefully assures that this information is not thrust at its members and their employers, that it is available as individuals choose to use it.

Special library salaries tend to be higher than those in other libraries. However, because librarians and information center professionals are a small subset of an organizational salary structure, there is wide variation. A personnel department usually can't be bothered to undertake intensive surveys to cover only a handful of individuals and is likely to assign librarians to an existing professional salary category. Further, salaries tend to increase more rapidly for individuals after employment in special libraries than in other kinds of libraries. This is again because special librarian salaries and increase percentages are normally tied to patterns established for other employees of the same organization. In the for-profit sector in particular, both starting salaries and salary increases tend to be higher than in the academic, school and public sectors in which most other librarians are found.

The Special Libraries Association, in its own annual salary update which involves a sampling of 25% of its membership, reported that the average (mean) salary for its members in 1983 in the United States was $26,489, an increase of 8.8% over the 1982 figure. This is a greater rate of increase than reported for other library groups or for the U.S. working population as a whole. Starting salary data reported annually in *Library Journal* by Carol Learmont and Stephen Van Houten also indicate that new graduates employed in special libraries are better paid. In 1982 the average beginning salary for all graduates was $16,583. For public librarians it was $15,006, for academic librarians $16,012, and for special librarians $17,681.

These specific figures are, of course, valid only for the years indicated, but there is no reason to doubt that the overall pattern will continue for the foreseeable future. Geographic patterns are also apparent, with starting salaries in the Northeast and Southwest generally higher than in other parts of the country. These differences are tied to regional salary patterns and probably also to the strong emphasis on science and technology libraries in the southwestern United States.

Similarly, benefits offered to special librarians are also those available to other professional employees. This means that medical and retirement benefits are usually better than in the academic and municipal sectors and that support for continuing education and other professional development is frequently greater. On the other hand, vacations are more frugally administered. Most corporations still start new employees with two weeks of vacation and increase this total only after a period of five to eight years of service. Special librarians who change jobs frequently rarely earn much vacation, and retirement benefits are usually not vested until after a certain number of years, in comparison to academia, where they are usually portable.

Working hours in special library settings are a little more predictable than in other libraries. While the collection may be available to its users on weekends and in the evenings, it is generally not staffed. All professionals recognize the responsibility of occasionally working late or on weekends to meet a deadline, but the kind of seven-day schedules so common in public libraries are not the norm. Special librarians will argue that they work more regulated hours, but that they work more intensively and under greater time pressures while they do work, and as a generalization this is probably true.

Despite wide variances, special librarians and information specialists who work in the corporate sector tend to be better paid, not because of a greater appreciation for them in these organizations, but rather because it is easier to adapt to existing comparable salary patterns for similar professional posts. Special librarians are well served when they tie their own salary structures to those already used for the professionals in heaviest demand in that organization. Special librarians with a masters degree and no experience will not suffer if they are paid at the same rates as economists with the same background in banks, or chemists, engineers or accountants in equivalent settings. Tying the library staff's fortunes to that star will not only serve the staff well but will also save the personnel department a bothersome, and to them trivial, problem.

Special librarians in the not-for-profit sector do not always have the same flexibility and availability of options. It is unfortunate that when a profession acquires the description of being "dedicated," this can become a synonym for underpaid—and that this tactic is used by personnel administrators in some nonprofit settings. Clearly one of the negotiating advantages of the corporate librarian is that the parent organization is not operating out of altruism, and there is nothing wrong in expecting a wage related to the value of services delivered.

CONCLUSION

It is understandable that special librarians have been reluctant to promulgate specific standards, let alone attempt to force them on organizations that have special libraries and information centers. The settings are all different and cannot be generalized, and there is also an unwillingness to prescribe when some entrepreneurial library managers would prefer to innovate without constraints. At the same time, it is also unfortunate that organizational managers, particularly corporate managers, are not provided at least with some indications of what they should expect and demand. The SLA consultation service attempts to do this, but since it only responds to specific invitations, the impact is limited.

These factors provide yet additional reasons for the special librarian to define the appropriate level of information service and not wait for the clientele to describe it. Years of observation have convinced this writer that there is virtually no level of special library service so poor and unresponsive that users will not rationalize it as "acceptable"—that is, until the next budget crunch. Then they may eliminate it entirely, because "after all it doesn't really do much." Succeeding chapters of this book will discuss both methods for the determination of necessary and high levels of information service and tactics for achieving them within the political environment in which special libraries and information centers exist.

SUGGESTED ADDITIONAL READINGS

Cowgill, Logan O. and Robert J. Havlik. "Standards for Special Libraries." *Library Trends* 21: 249-260 (October 1972).

Dodd, James B. "The Gap in Standards for Special Libraries." *Library Trends* 31:85-91 (Summer 1982).

Special Libraries Association. "Objectives and Standards for Special Libraries." *Special Libraries* 55:672-680 (December 1964). Also issued as *Objectives for Special Libraries*. New York: Special Libraries Association, 1970.

Special Libraries Association. *SLA Triennial Salary Survey*. New York: Special Libraries Association, 1983. (Planned for repetition every three years.)

Stinson, E. Ray. "Standards for Health Sciences Libraries." *Library Trends* 31:125-137 (Summer 1982).

5

Acquiring and Distributing Library Materials

At a minimum any reasonably adequate special library does two things: It owns some things for immediate and direct use, and it purchases and borrows other things for which the need arises. It is disturbing that a great many libraries do exactly this and nothing more, and even more disturbing that many users find this level of service perfectly acceptable. (This passivity toward information and library services, well described by sociologist George Shapiro in several talks at Special Libraries Association meetings, may have its genesis in early and constricting experiences dating back to childhood and the public or school library.) As a consultant, this writer has met high-level executives who express gratitude for the "favor" of the librarian's willingness to take the trouble to borrow what the library does not already possess, forgetting that the provision of service to them and others is really the library's only reason for existence.

Given this level of passivity, it is not startling that some of these individuals accept delays of up to two months as "reasonable." Of course, the painful reverse side of this process comes in the fact that when that delay is *not* acceptable, they don't necessarily complain. Either they pretend they didn't need the material at all, in another validation of Mooers' Law, or they find their own way around the system. The reader should never forget that there are usually two reasons for the user's acceptance of low levels of service. One is based on the lack of a historical basis for expectations, the other on the knowledge that there are other alternatives open.

DEVELOPING THE COLLECTION

The development of a library collection, constrained as it is by both space and budgetary limitations, should be based on a best estimate of what will be needed. This approach differs from that of major academic libraries, which may purchase materials that have no predetermined "usefulness" but may, some day, be of interest to scholars. Special library materials are presumably in the collection because they have been or will be used.

Building an adequate library in the presence of space constraints requires that material that is not needed—because it is obsolete, because it never should have been bought in the first place, because organizational needs have changed—should be removed by being given away or thrown away. On the other hand, if material is needed and there is not enough room, then options of off-site storage and microfilming of less frequently used materials or back runs of journals should be considered. (Operations research studies tell us that rigorous weeding should take place even when there is plenty of space, because it is harder to find what you are looking for in a larger collection than in a smaller one.) A special library, to be most effective, should be as large as it need be and no larger.

Considerations of what must be bought are also affected by the ability to access materials in other files and other locations, the speed and cost of doing this, the cost to the library in terms of manpower allocations and the needs of the users. On the other hand, purchase decisions should never be controlled by the adequacy of space. Confront or spotlight that problem as necessary, but don't allow the tail to wag the dog.

Sources of Materials

In developing an information collection, special librarians are not necessarily always constrained by the cost of the material itself, although the cost of acquisition, processing, analysis and storage is not inconsequential, and special libraries should never acquire material just because it is free or offered. However, much useful information can be obtained from government publications, which used to be free and are still reasonably cheap. Other significant sources include materials from vendors and suppliers and, most importantly, information generated within the organization itself. Countless observations have shown both that internal material is frequently the most useful and heavily demanded and that for a variety of reasons, including the originator's desire to control access, it is sometimes the most difficult to acquire.

Size of the Collection

In starting a new library, a new collection must be developed. In continuing an existing collection, ongoing policies—if in fact there are any—must be evaluated. Objectives for what the collection is designed to achieve must be developed and presented to management because, as already pointed out, management rarely has expectations and even more rarely is in a position to quantify them.

As a minimum, the most passive of special libraries needs a collection that will be able to respond to some portion of the questions that are asked and to supply some percentage of the material that is requested. How large a portion? That answer depends in part on the accessibility of other resources—other libraries within the organization or major collections readily available within a walking distance of a few blocks. The more difficult it is to obtain material from other sources, the more expensive it becomes, the more time and effort it involves, and the greater the extent of inability to meet the time constraints of the clientele, the more self-sufficient the collection should be.

It must again be stressed that we have been discussing only a reactive collection, one which responds to requests that are in large part unsolicited. Special library managers can indeed create an interest in certain fields—for example, the development of a management reading program, which will create further needs that must be met. Fundamentally, growth is accomplished not through the process of always satisfying existing needs, but by creating new needs, which in turn require additional resources and programs. That is the entrepreneurial aspect that so characterizes special librarianship: the planned fostering of dissatisfaction, with an accompanying plan to deal with that dissatisfaction. Students of organizational dynamics will recognize this as risk management. It is progress through the planned and controlled creation of crises, followed by their solution.

The special librarian will undoubtedly have to come up with some sort of target for the adequacy of the collection, stated in terms of the ability to satisfy document requests. In the experience of this writer, a figure of between 50% and 75% will appear reasonable to corporate management. Fortunately, a relatively small but carefully selected collection can achieve this target. Samuel C. Bradford, a British librarian and bibliographer, postulated in the 1930s that a geometric increase in collection size was required to achieve an arithmetic growth in service response and formulated what has come to be known as "Bradford's Law." Richard W. Trueswell, Professor of Industrial Engineering and Operations Research at the University of Massachusetts, stated this relationship more succinctly in 1969, when he formulated and demonstrated the 80/20 rule: 80% of requests are satisfied from 20% of the collection. It follows from this that even fractional increases above the suggested level of 75% self-sufficiency become an elusive and expensive target.

Levels of Acquisitions

There are four levels of acquisitions of materials:

1. Material is purchased as users request (or demand) it.

2. In addition to this, suggestions are solicited and welcome.

3. In addition to these, the library asks specific users to evaluate the desirability of acquiring materials that have come to the attention of the library staff.

4. The library purchases material or places subscriptions on its own cognizance.

While these approaches are not mutually exclusive, only a library staff making full use of the last alternative can hope to develop an adequately responsive collection. Only in this way can needs in new areas of interest be anticipated. Only the special librarian can determine what has had to be borrowed repeatedly on interlibrary loan or what journals are included in data bases that are frequently accessed and are therefore likely to be requested.

Finally, only the librarian can assure balance in the collection. Users will obviously recommend or ask for materials in their own fields, and an aggressively active user can soak up the library materials budget by creating strengths totally out of keeping with organizational priorities. By contrast, the library staff must protect the informational interests of groups that do not take an active interest in material selection. Frequently these people are the key senior management.

Academic libraries also face this problem; sometimes they deal with it by allocating percentages of the materials budget to certain areas of interest. However, since these allocations are normally based on history rather than on need, they also have their imperfections. In the final analysis, only the library and information center staff can make the determination that an excellent book can be ignored because its contribution to collection coverage would be superfluous, while a less highly regarded work may fill a nagging gap. Users can tell you whether a work is good, but not whether or not it is needed.

The Problem of Classified Documents

Those special librarians whose collections involve acquisition of government reports with security classifications may encounter a problem with internal security officers, which concerns not dollars but the "need to know." Many special librarians have excellent relationships with their security officers. Some do not, however, and must fight for their authority to build collections in anticipation of need.

Fundamentally, librarians and security officers have priorities as antithetical as those of the mongoose and the cobra. Librarians want to assure that all needed information is accessible to anyone who wants or needs it. Security officers want to assure that unauthorized documents are not distributed, and they can fulfill that responsibility even if, in the process, authorized and needed documents are also not distributed. That is not their problem—in the ultimate "secure" system nobody sees anything.

MAKING THE COLLECTION AVAILABLE

Having acquired an adequate collection, the special library must also take steps to assure that the materials are indeed available when wanted or needed.

Departmental Materials and the Special Library

Many libraries acquire materials directly for permanent retention in departmental offices. This is not unreasonable, since the library is most familiar with ordering routines and discounts. The establishment of rudimentary bibliographic control can assure that organizational ownership is retained and that the material can be accessed when someone else needs to see it. The rarity of such a need is assumed, because otherwise the library would presumably have bought its own copy. It is further assumed that while the library may act as purchasing agent, library funds will not be involved.

There is certainly legitimacy in all of these actions. Some materials, such as perhaps legal works in a technical library, legitimately belong in only one office. Other materials, such as handbooks that are in frequent use, may be required in multiple copies to avoid the need to go to the library every time they are wanted.

Nevertheless, even in this process, some warnings should be heeded. If the expenditures for personal materials exceed those for general library materials, it may be an indication of an affluent or generous management—or of a vacillating one. However, if large sums are expended for departmental or individual books or subscriptions while the library's own budget is kept in tight check, something is very wrong. Not only are the organization's funds being spent unwisely, but alternatives to the use of the library are being developed, and this is something to which all special library managers must be constantly alert. There are some librarians who encourage user groups to purchase books and subscriptions so that the library won't have to spend its own funds. Such an action certainly avoids being confrontational, but it is just as surely suicidal.

Requested Materials

Some books and documents, although acquired with library funds, may have been initially requested by an individual user, and it is therefore not unreasonable to let this individual have first use. For how long? For as long as it takes the user to skim it, read it or determine he really wants his own copy—certainly not more than a month. Any longer period simply creates an alternative to the departmentally purchased copy: a "free" book for the department, paid for by the library. Academic libraries suffer from the problem of having their best materials located in faculty offices. Special libraries, with much smaller collections, cannot afford this. The commonly held misperception that materials sitting in offices for a period of several years are "being used" is obviously absurd.

The special library cannot force the return of materials which it owns but which users insist they still need, six months or two years later. It cannot win an argument over the question of what someone needs to do his or her job. However, the library can insist that since its copy is now being retained on what is effectively permanent loan, a second copy will have to be purchased and budgeted to the department in question. Not only do users find this fair, so do accountants.

The Shelf Collection

The point of all of this is not to establish tighter location controls. (Since this is invariably assumed, the need to refute that charge can be anticipated.) The point is to develop a collection of materials good enough so that individuals can visit the library in the expectation that something of value will be there. Recalling the material on request does not serve that purpose, because many individuals do not know whether or not they really need a particular item until they have glanced at it. If this requires recalling the item from somebody who presumably is "using it" (obviously a slow reader), then they won't bother.

Maintaining a quality shelf collection by insisting that material either be returned or a replacement purchased helps reverse what is otherwise a self-fulfilling prophecy. Often individuals don't return things because they fear that the item will be not be available if and when they need it again. They retain it for their own security, and of course others do the same. By contrast, if users are confident that materials will be available, they will also return things more readily. Sometimes library users understand this process better than librarians. This author, on a consulting assignment, once asked a chemist why he never visited the library to look for material which might be of interest. The chemist responded that he did not do so because the library collection was "self-selected junk." Anything worth reading was in someone's office, and that is where he began his search.

Journals and Routing Lists

The scattering and resultant disappearance of library materials also includes current issues of journals, which in some libraries are routed to a list of 10 or more readers. Journal routing is a slow and ineffective technique, particularly if titles of current interest such as weeklies are involved and don't reach the last reader until months later. Journal routing sometimes gives the appearance of effectiveness to high-level descision makers, because these individuals sit at the top of the routing list and have no problems. For others, the situation is poor. Not only is the process slow, but also many journals disappear and never reach their intended total audience, let alone return to the library. In addition, current issues are never available in the central place we are encouraging individuals to frequent.

For users who have difficulty in visiting the library, the routing of title pages or of commercially developed contents journals is usually preferable, with the library or information center assuring that needed copies can be requested at any time in the process. Libraries must, of course, comply with provisions of the copyright law, but such compliance should never be an excuse for depriving individuals of needed copies. The cost is too trivial to warrant the inconvenience. The copyright law was never intended even by its staunchest advocates to eliminate copying, only to assure payment for the service. If journals must be routed, because of user idiosycrasy or geographic distance, the library should arrange multiple subscriptions. Users should have the assurance that if they visit the library at least once a week, the latest issues of all periodicals will be available for them to read and, if necessary, to copy specific articles under proper legal restraints. In addition, they should also find a pretty good shelf collection of books they might want to scan.

OBTAINING NON-LIBRARY MATERIALS

As already noted, at least 25% of the materials that individuals want will not be part of the library's collection, but have to be obtained elsewhere, through purchase or loan. It is important that mechanisms for doing this rapidly are developed. The interlibrary loan procedures developed within the library community are geared to cooperation and economy but not to speed. Response times of four weeks and longer are not unusual, and these are intolerable for the time frame in which the special library operates. Overnight delivery services have proliferated, and special libraries make heavy use of them, trading dollars for speed.

It is perhaps startling but true that the cheapest commodity in virtually all special libraries is money. Even in tightly constrained libraries it is normally in greater supply than either manpower or time. A study being completed by a doctoral student at Indiana University examines the alternatives selected by special librarians when materials are needed from other organizations and contrasts these strategies with those employed by more traditional libraries. The use of messengers to pick up and deliver, requests by telephone or teletype, which bypass the multicarbon interlibrary loan form, and the reliance on commercial delivery services are not uncommon. Moreover, they are totally appropriate.

Interlibrary loan and other types of cooperative services will be discussed more fully in Chapter 11.

PROMOTING THE COLLECTION

Even in the most passive and reactive special library setting, a way must be found to inform users of newly acquired material. This is usually accomplished through the distribution of a library bulletin. Normally a bulletin is produced monthly, which immediately suggests some potential problems. A month may be a long time to wait, or a monthly bulletin of 25 or more pages may be too time-consuming for the clientele to read unless its arrangement into subject categories provides a more simplified access. However, with the increasingly interdisciplinary nature of project interests, compartmentalization becomes more difficult.

Effective Bulletins

Regardless of format, any announcement bulletin should list all available materials. It should certainly include reports and pamphlets, particularly those generated within the organization. It should indicate new journal titles subscribed to, new data bases available for access and bibliographies compiled by the staff. This last has the double advantage of disseminating information while at the same time pointing to professional activities that have been undertaken.

The bulletin should be distributed to all appropriate professional personnel, not just the ones who ask to see it. It should most definitely be sent to general management. If there is a lack of interest at that level, the solution is not to stop sending it but to make the publication of greater interest.

Dissemination with greater frequency is advisable, just to keep the name and telephone number of the library in front of the user's face. If the library distributes tables of contents of newly received periodicals, weekly circulation is most certainly appropriate. The cost is trivial, but that doesn't mean it won't be questioned. It is one of the characteristics of management controls, as so correctly expressed by C. Northcote Parkinson, that the amount of time spent in scrutinizing an activity is inversely proportional to its importance (or its cost).

It goes almost without saying that any bulletin should include easy mechanisms for requesting listed material. Asking the user to return a marked-up copy of a bulletin is not always effective, particularly when supervisors share it with their groups. It would be preferable to provide for each reader the opportunity to request material directly—by telephone, because this is still the preferred and most effective means of communication in special libraries, or by a separate order form that can be used to request books, reports or copies of articles.

When Marjorie Griffin managed the IBM library at San Jose, CA, she distributed a daily bulletin. It included library announcements and also news of meetings and seminars, visitors, birthdays and anniversaries. There were also short pieces of poetry or prose, usually of a humorous nature, some of it contributed by employees. Finally, and very importantly in an organization with a stock option plan, it included the closing price of IBM stock. All of these are tactics for making individuals aware of the library and its services.

Other Techniques

Increasingly, special libraries and information centers are taking advantage of the fact that the easy availability of computer terminals permits direct access to library bibliographic holdings from the user's own office. New accessions can be listed on the computers' "bulletin board," and libraries can develop electronic message systems through which individuals can request library service. Failing that, the library should at least have a telephone answering machine on which recorded messages can be left.

While the library should encourage direct contact with its users and facilitate that contact both through the provision of attractive facilities and a shelf collection worth looking at, much of the contact will come by mail, by telephone or through electronic messages, from individuals who consider themselves too busy or who are at inconvenient distances. The author once managed a centralized information center with direct service responsibilities for individuals in 56 separate building locations, some in other cities or in other countries. Obviously, strategies for reaching such individuals must be adapted to what works.

PROVIDING SEARCH SERVICES

Almost all special libraries presently undertake bibliographies and other less formal methods for retrospective search. It is the belief of this writer that as bibliographic access and even the ability to order documents directly become easier from the user's own office or home, bibliographic services will become the bread and butter of library services. The library that fails to meet and encourage this need will be in considerable difficulty.

Much has been written lately on whether users will want to conduct their own bibliographic searches or will turn to information intermediaries in the library or information center. All of what has been written is speculative because there really aren't any hard numbers. Much of it is also self-serving. One might assume that those who develop and market data bases would want to encourage direct individual use, both for the additional funds and for prestige.

Ultimately, this writer is quite certain that our clientele will not pay the slightest attention to suggestions of what they ought to do; they will do what is most comfortable for them. Some will undoubtedly find the idea of conducting their own information inquiries fascinating, a few for the rest of their productive lives, others for about a month until the novelty wears off. Many others will happily delegate the search process to the library, if they have reason to trust that a satisfactory job will be done and if there are no suggestions from the staff that such delegation is unreasonable and that users should really do this work themselves. Such policies are commonplace in academic libraries, but they have no place in the special library, whose only reason for existence is what it is able to accomplish to facilitate the work of others.

CONCLUSION

Up to now we have dealt only with the development of reactive services, although suggestions have been included for making even this relatively low level of service positively viewed and well received. In Chapter 6, we will consider ways to develop a higher level of service to meet organizational needs, including the use of computer-based technologies. The assumption is that this higher level of service is what is really wanted and needed, and what will earn support, appreciation and credit.

However, even in the offering of reactive services, the library manager must look for warning signs that indicate trouble or the potential for trouble. Nature abhors a vacuum, and organizational dynamics exhibit very natural tendencies. If a lack of support for library activities leads to a low level of information flow, that is bad enough. If your failure or inability to provide needed services leads to the development of alternatives—when individuals or groups establish informal libraries of their own, when they purchase materials because you can't afford to, when they access data bases or make direct purchases from vendors or information brokers—you are really in trouble, and you must recognize the cause of that difficulty.

The cause is not money, because the money is being spent. What has happened is that you have lost control over your area of responsibility, over your organizational "turf." It may follow quite logically that if potential users can dispense with you some of the time, they may decide they can dispense with you all of the time. This point will be explored in greater detail in later chapters.

SUGGESTED ADDITIONAL READINGS

Boss, Richard W. "The Library as an Information Broker." *College & Research Libraries* 40:136-140 (March 1979).

Dodd, James B. "Information Brokers." *Special Libraries* 67:243-250 (May-June 1976).

Garvin, David. "The Information Analysis Center and the Library." *Special Libraries* 62:17-23 (January 1971).

Newman, Wilda B. "Managing a Report Collection for Zero Growth." *Special Libraries* 71:276-282 (May-June 1980).

Special Libraries: A Guide for Management, Second Edition. Op. cit.

Trueswell, Richard W. "Some Behavioral Patterns of Library Users: The 80/20 Rule." *Wilson Library Bulletin* 44:458-461 (January 1969).

6

User Expectations and Enhanced Services

In order to provide more than basic, reactive service, the library manager must make clients aware of the enhanced professional services that the library can and should perform. Clients are already well aware of the library's clerical activities. Even researchers, who are experienced library users and may make heavy demands, often stress the clerical tasks of book ordering, journal routing and interlibrary borrowing of specific articles (perhaps as identified for them in a data base search by another "professional" organization). Users outside the research group, particularly those in organizations such as marketing, accounting, production and public relations—very frequently the key individuals in any organization—have little expectation that the library exists to serve them at all and so ask for little.

PROBLEMS OF LOW EXPECTATIONS

In situations where the collection and service are developed simply in response to expressed demands, low expectations become a self-fulfilling prophecy.

Expectations of Self-Service

Users have been indoctrinated, in their passage through the educational system, to believe that the use of a library is largely a self-service process and that they will be criticized if they are unable to pass this "test." What results is yet another variant of Mooers' Law, in which individuals who are unable to find what they need and unwilling to admit their need for professional help will pretend they didn't need any help at all. Those who have worked in academic and public libraries are familiar with the phenomenon of people who walk in somewhat hesitatingly, briefly look around the stacks or open a few catalog drawers, and then leave. It happens in special libraries, too.

Good reference librarians are taught to be alert to such instances and to approach such individuals to create the clear impression that the responsibility for a successful service connection is not the user's, but the library's. Of course, sometimes the reference librarian is already busy with another client or on the telephone, and can only watch helplessly while an unserved potential user—who may not as a result be an enemy but who certainly won't be a supporter—disappears around the corner.

Attitudes of Librarians

On the other hand, some librarians really do think that their responsibility ends with the provision of a collection and the symbolic ringing of a bell to connote "come and get it." Such attitudes are transmitted in the shocked questions, "Don't you know how to use a catalog?" or "Didn't they teach you how to use the indexes when you went to school?" Many users, intimidated by libraries from their childhood experiences, will slink away, determined never to return if they can avoid it—and of course they can.

This attitude has even been expressed by the dean of a major school of library education, who stated at a conference that he saw the special library's role only as one of providing a strong collection; whether or not it was properly used was not the library's problem. Special librarians and would-be special librarians should dissociate themselves from such a viewpoint. Nevertheless, this perception persists among users, and it must be rooted out through the continued insistence that helping users is the librarian's responsibility, and if they are not helped, that becomes the librarian's failure.

User Insecurity

Chapter 2 noted that the development of special libraries was heavily concentrated in the United States and other western nations. Some of that is undoubtedly due to a higher degree of industrialization and information sophistication. However, there is another, more subtle factor. Special library and information service cannot exist unless there is a willingness on the part of users to admit there are things they don't know. Only then can they be served.

In societies in which such an admission is not acceptable, Mooers' Law becomes pervasive. International travelers know that in some countries a request for directions will always yield directions (even if they are wrong) because the person being asked is reluctant to admit he or she doesn't know. Individuals with such insecurities don't make good special library users.

Lack of Trust

There is also a commonly held perception that users' problems are so complex that the librarian couldn't possibly understand them. This phenomenon is well understood by all reference librarians as the process of question negotiation. We know that most users will tend to phrase what they really want to know in terms simpler than the actual question. In a public library a patron might, for instance, request material about wood rather than about the construction of a summer log cabin. In special libraries the phenomenon leads to computer search questions that are far too general, far too inclusive and, as a result, both useless and expensive. A partial solution has been to insist on hiring librarians and information specialists who also have advanced subject degrees, but that is not always possible and isn't really the answer, anyway. The answer, as discussed later in this chapter, is in the opening of one-to-one personal communications that not only erase the forbidding image of the library but also instill in users the sense of confidence that they can be helped. Ultimately, successful performance becomes the only criterion to warrant further business.

It is perfectly natural that users will seek out not the organization but the one specific individual in it who has helped them before. As a special library administrator, this writer has had a user refuse to tell him his question, preferring to return next week when "his" reference librarian will be back from vacation. This is not an insult; in fact, it is a perfectly acceptable situation, so long as there is some staff member the user does trust.

BARRIERS TO ENHANCED SERVICES: THE INDIANA SURVEY

Special librarians complain that they cannot help clients who do not come at all or who send their inquiries through surrogates or in garbled form. A survey undertaken in the 1970s by the Indiana chapter of the Special Libraries Association, in which 46 libraries participated, gives some indication of library frustration. As might be expected, there is some unhappiness with the level of resource allocation as expressed in dollars, staff size and space. However, other concerns of equal and even greater importance relate to problems in the interaction among librarians, library users and upper-level management. These problems have their roots in a failure to communicate, particularly the failure by librarians to make it clear what they could accomplish if only given the opportunity to perform effectively.

Difficulties with Patrons

The problem mentioned most frequently by the respondents, and stated as the greatest concern by 35% of them, was difficulties with patrons. These will be discussed here in descending order of their importance to the respondents. First are problems caused by questions passing to the library through a third person, usually a secretary who knows the specific question but doesn't understand the context. The all-important process of question negotiation is foreclosed. Why don't the users come to the library directly? Because they are too "busy," because the question isn't worth their direct intervention, or because they don't feel comfortable in the library? Probably some or all of the above.

The second complaint concerns the fact that users don't know what the library can do. This concern has been discussed previously, and there is really only one solution in dealing with such users. Tell them, in groups or individually—and repeatedly! Third is that users don't bring all of the needed information when they ask for help. Sometimes this can be dealt with. For example, if they really do know the exact citation but forgot to write it down, perhaps they can be trained. However, other inexact queries stem from a hazy recollection, and if we convey to users that only perfectly framed questions can be accepted, we will lose a great deal of our value. Good reference librarians, of course, pride themselves on their ability to work with fragmented and sometimes totally misleading clues.

The fourth complaint concerns a lack of communication during the search process. A lengthy endeavor such as a literature search might, in a special library, take several weeks and in some instances several months. There is obviously danger in such a situation, because the search may be heading in the wrong direction, particularly if specifications were incompletely delivered. However, the solution to this problem is also obvious. If the user doesn't seek out the library, the library must seek out the user, with status reports and inquiries. One of the strategies to be discussed later in this chapter requires that the library manager find or make the time to get out of the library to interact with users in their own offices and laboratories. This is not an imposition if the manager is businesslike and to the point; in fact, it is part of the job. Of course, if users think when they see the librarian coming that it is to recover an overdue book (because that is the only reason anyone ever appears), the visitor won't be very welcome.

The final complaint under this general heading concerns a lack of feedback, a failure to communicate whether what was provided was of value. This is frustrating not only because librarians, like others, need approbation as well as criticism, but also because they need reactions to improve future service. Some failure to respond is willful, but most of it is just thoughtlessness. After all, users are also very busy. There is really only one cure: you must ask for feedback, and you must explain that you need feedback to improve future service.

Relations with Management

The second general area of complaint, mentioned as the primary area of concern by 16% of the respondents, concerns relations with administration. These problems involve lack of interest on the part of management, which has already been noted, and a lack of communication, which largely results from that lack of interest. In turn, lack of communication results in the failure to provide the advance information special librarians obviously need if they are to provide anticipatory services.

There is only one solution to this problem, and it is directly confrontational. Special librarians complain that they receive no information because they are very low on the organization chart, and that is frequently true. However, it is also totally irrelevant, because every chain of command ultimately reaches the same top level. If the librarian is not being informed of what he or she needs to know, then this is a failing of a higher level of management, and management must be informed of this shortcoming, politely and reasonably if possible (at least at first). After all, communication of needed information will improve the performance of subordinate units, and fundamentally it costs nothing. Of course, the demand must be specific, identifying what needs to be known and is not now being communicated.

Bibliographic Problems

The third area of concern, considered primary by 14% of the respondents, involves bibliographic problems. Such difficulties may include a lack of indexing depth or the reverse, indexes that are too sophisticated. There may also be problems with terminology. Bibliographic problems, while serious, are outside the scope of this book, which emphasizes management relationships. However, special librarians are heavily dependent on intensely subject-oriented material, some of which is indexed and abstracted by professional societies in the subject field. Many of these (with the notable exception of some major organizations such as the American Chemical Society and its publication *Chemical Abstracts*) pay no attention to the fact that many if not most of the primary users of their publications are not subject specialists. There is no total solution to this problem. Partial solutions involve complaints, publicity and perhaps some financial pressure.

Lack of Staff and Funds

The next area, mentioned as primary by 12% of the respondents, concerns a lack of staff and funds. It might be surprising that the ranking is so low, since the literature suggests this is the primary complaint of academic and particularly of public librarians. In the special libraries represented in the Indiana survey, a lack of budgetary support translated most directly into a lack of staff, particularly into a shortage of clerks.

It is one of the significant characteristics of special libraries that personnel hiring ceilings often are superimposed on budgetary ceilings; these are particularly difficult to change when it comes to hiring clerks. It is unfortunately also one of the characteristics of librarianship that clerical work in libraries take precedence over professional work. In the absence of clerks, professionals perform clerical duties. This is a waste of resources, it is demoralizing for those prepared to do more, and it perpetuates the impression of librarians as overly educated clerks. It is a problem that must be fought with reason, logic and evidence of wasteful expenditure. When absolutely essential, the problem can be spotlighted by leaving the unstaffed clerical duties undone. (Chapter 12 will consider the issue of professional versus clerical tasks in greater detail.)

Last on this list of shortages is the materials budget. This is not totally surprising. Organizations that support nothing else, whose view of the library is totally as a self-service operation, will support a materials budget, if not for the library itself then certainly for the user groups. It must be remembered that the start of many, if not most, special libraries comes from the fact that the materials budget or at least materials expenditures were there first, and the staff becomes the afterthought, to "tend" the collection.

Library Networks and Communications

The next area of concern, expressed as primary by 10% of respondents, involves communications and relations with other libraries and with networks. This concern, which will be addressed further in Chapter 11, derives from the facts both that special libraries have unique problems, which usually center more on speed and accuracy than on cost, and that most networks and cooperative arrangements were not developed with special librarians in mind. Indeed, in some cases there was question and concern about whether these not-for-profit consortia and cooperatives could serve libraries in the for-profit sector.

Other Concerns

Two other concerns were revealed by the survey. For 9.5% of the respondents, lack of time was the most important concern. Here some level of interpretation is required. Special libraries do work under greater time pressures, because their users do. This is one of the characteristics that identifies special librarianship; at least to some extent, it must simply be accepted as a fact. However, if lack of time results from a lack of staff, and particularly if professionals are too busy doing clerical work to do their own, or if a lack of time results from a failure to receive advance information that could have been provided, lack of time is not just a catch-all concern but a symptom of serious problems.

Only 3.5% of Indiana chapter respondents mentioned a lack of adequate space as their primary concern. This is somewhat surprising and may simply be a characteristic of the membership of this group. Perhaps respondents in more urban locations, such as New York City, where space is expensive, might have answered differently. In general, space is usually either no problem at all or a very great problem, whose dimensions sometimes eclipse even the continuing concerns about dollars and people.

IMPLICATIONS OF THE SURVEY

The Indiana survey indicates quite clearly that inadequate support for the special library results not from inadequate funding but from other problems. These are the failure to establish a meaningful professional relationship with users and the failure to open similar communications channels with management. The second problem will be addressed in Chapter 9, but to a large extent the two concerns are related. First, managers are also users, or at least they could be and ought to be. Second, managers will care about inadequacies if enough users express a concern.

Turning Complaints into Higher Expectations

It may be difficult to get users to express any feelings of expectation or dissatisfaction. When such comments are forthcoming, they usually focus on perceived disenchantment with clerical service levels. It takes too long to order a book, the staff keeps nagging them about overdue materials, requested photocopies are late, etc. Management reactions to such complaints rarely include an increase in clerical support for the library. The prejudice against clerical overhead expenditures is simply too strong. Rather, it usually involves greater pressure on librarians to get the clerical work done, predictably by suggesting or dictating that the professionals do it themselves.

The expression of user dissatisfaction can be productive, but it must be solicited and channeled to concentrate on professional services—on reference work, on literature searches, on current awareness, on analytical surveys and bulletins. This is not easily accomplished if users are not aware that such services can be provided and that librarians can provide them. It becomes even more difficult if the users have been told during their school days (sometimes by librarians) that it is lazy and unprofessional to request such assistance.

Fighting Indifference

To bring users to an increased level of expectations and demands requires a subtle and individualized approach. Users must be cultivated through one-to-one contacts, and that means the library or information center manager has to get out of his or her office and into theirs. The assumption that users are too busy to talk to you is nonsense. Properly approached, and at a time when they are not facing crucial and immediate deadlines of their own, people like nothing better than to talk about their work. (In fact, it is one of their great frustrations that nobody cares—not their boss, not their spouse, certainly not their children.)

The premise for this discussion is based on your need, not theirs. It is your need to do your job by finding out how the library can serve them. Individuals who do not use the library blame themselves, and never the library, for not having what they want. This sort of tractability underlies the problem with the many surveys that have asked individuals what they thought about library service. The questionnaires inevitably evoke favorable responses, because individuals adapt their own answers to what they think will be considered "reasonable." Only when they are asked to make ranking decisions involving the library and other services competing for budgetary support do they respond in terms of whether the library is important to them and the way they work.

Truly useful surveys question not only heavy users but also nonusers and include queries designed to probe beneath the protective shield that is invariably raised. For example: If you are not using the library, why aren't you? Do you have information needs you wish someone could address—and for the moment don't worry about whether or not such a request is reasonable?

The phenomenon of user acceptance of low-level service as "reasonable" has been with us a long time. It is to some extent puzzling because these same users exhibit no such tolerance for improperly cooked food in the cafeteria, unfilled potholes in front of their houses or misdelivered mail. Librarians pay a great price for this acquiescence. In a talk delivered to a group of junior mechanical engineers more than 20 years ago, this author suggested that they not put up with inferior library service. Demanding good service would either support the library manager, who had been making the same point all along, or expose an incompetent, who should be terminated. These junior engineers are now senior engineers, and it is obvious they haven't paid the slightest attention.

POTENTIAL FOR SERVICE

The inability of our users to see obvious connections cannot be exaggerated. Individuals who receive and are gratified by the compilation of periodic bibliographies are sometimes surprised to learn that the same computer search can be performed monthly against an incremental data base and called SDI (selective dissemination of information). They fail to connect slow interlibrary loan response time with the obvious suggestions that the library find some other institutions that respond more rapidly or explore other means of delivery or perhaps buy more, in anticipation of requests.

We are still talking about information services that result in the delivery of documents, although in their more sophisticated states they become more aggressively defined services that seek out rather than wait for the user. Information services that deal in information packaging or even information analysis open yet another realm.

Information Packaging

Information packaging is certainly simple enough. The development of a monthly report listing competitor activities as drawn from *The New York Times Index* requires no great skill, if you know who your competitors are. The library staff can do this quite easily. However, in many organizations with which this writer is familiar, there are groups of highly paid subject area professionals who do nothing more complex than this. A biomedical alerting service staffed by doctors listed articles on diabetes, as indexed by the National Library of Medicine's *Index Medicus*, and distributed it worldwide. This certainly does not require a subject professional; it may not even require a professional librarian. Yet, the perception persists that librarians cannot do this, or even worse, that they won't because "they are too busy." Doing what?

Information Analysis

The development of analytical services is yet another dimension. Alvin Weinberg of the Oak Ridge National Laboratory suggested almost 30 years ago that professional scientists needed to become more actively involved with their literature, not only to index and abstract it but to evaluate it to tell the potential reader whether or not it was worth reading. During the more affluent 1960s, a number of such information analysis centers came into being. Few have survived the need to justify their costs in terms of benefits provided, and those still in existence are heavily subsidized. It may be that the task is just too difficult, and that it is not possible for one individual in one location to determine what someone else may find of interest.

If the process were simple, SDI profile responses would approach 100%, and 80% positive response would not be considered an excellent level. It may be that for some situations a negative response, one which adds no additional information, is an important search conclusion. That is certainly true in many patent searches, where we hope to find nothing in order to support our own claim of originality. Finally, it may be that the subject professionals willing to work at this activity are not the ones whose subject knowledge is considered completely reliable.

Whatever the reasons, the provision of information analysis services is still beyond the capabilities of most special libraries and information centers. It is possible that this task will become a more realistic one in the next 20 years. If that occurs, then obviously the staffing of special libraries will have to change. Chapter 13, at the close of this book, will examine some of these potential future developments.

CONCLUSION

For the moment, there is plenty of room for most libraries to raise the expectations of both management and users for an information service that is largely still based on document delivery and on specific answers. Such service is primarily reactive and responsive but can move beyond this to the delivery of materials and answers that are needed although they may never have been requested. Finally, there are opportunities for information packaging, in the continuing recognition that the library serves extremely busy individuals. Most would prefer to receive less information than they presently receive; thus, expanding the volume of service does not help them. However, they would like what they get to be more directly applicable and, even better, to be already there for their use when they need it.

The suggestions above are general, and intentionally so. No two special libraries are alike, and no two user groups exhibit similar characteristics and problems. For these reasons, no specific program can be prescribed. Every special library manager has the immediate and urgent task of determining what the particular and unique needs of that library's clientele are. Waiting for users to ask for help will not deal with the problem, and sending out questionnaires inviting suggestions is little better. Such questionnaires are likely to result only in an endorsement of the present library service, poor as it may be. If anything, they will lead to suggestions that clerical activity be strengthened, diverting resources from professional activity.

Proposals for the initiation or enhancement of professional services must come from the library staff. They must be so phrased as to appear directly helpful, not threatening, to each individual user, and they must make it clear that strong professional library service is a right, not a privilege. If such an atmosphere can be created, management support is inevitable—not because management is anxious to spend more money, but because the expenditures in question are trivial compared to other budget items, and the potential benefits are great.

SUGGESTED ADDITIONAL READINGS

Bailey, Martha J. "Functions of Selected Company Libraries/Information Services." *Special Libraries* 72:18-30 (January 1981).

Bauer, Charles K. "Managing Management." *Special Libraries* 71:204-216 (April 1980).

Boaz, Martha. "Evaluation of Special Library Service for Upper Management." *Special Libraries* 59:789-791 (December 1968).

Curtis, John and Stephen Abram. "Special and Corporate Libraries: Planning for Survival and Success." *Canadian Library Journal* 40:225-228 (August 1983).

Kates, Jacqueline R. "One Measure of a Library's Contribution." *Special Libraries* 65:332-336 (August 1974).

Matarazzo, James M. "Lessons from the Past: Special Libraries in Times of Retrenchment." *Canadian Library Journal* 40:221-223 (August 1983).

Robertson, W. Davenport. "A User-Oriented Approach to Setting Priorities for Library Service." *Special Libraries* 71:345-353 (August 1980).

White, Herbert S. "Growing User Information Dependence and Its Impact on the Library Field." *ASLIB Proceedings* 31(2):74-87 (February 1979).

7

The Impact of Technology

In an effort to provide a higher level of service to users, the special library manager—like managers of academic and public libraries—is making increasing use of technology. This chapter will discuss some of the significant technological advances as they affect library service. It is not intended as a technical manual, nor as a "how-to-do-it" guide for operations, but rather as a way of alerting managers to the potential benefits and pitfalls of computer applications.

Automation by itself does not bring about successful libraries. If the wrong task is mechanized, or if a function already improperly performed in a manual system is thrown into a computer environment, the result may be more rapid or more efficient, but it is still the wrong operation. The phrase which most directly and aptly describes this phenomenon of improper computerization is expressed as GIGO (garbage in, garbage out).

Technology deserves particular mention in any work dealing with special libraries and information centers, primarily because these organizations have always been in the forefront of technological evaluation and application. This characteristic predates the development of computers. It applies, for example, to the development of specialized semiautomated document handling systems, such as Termatrex and Uniterm, and to the use of microforms and other reprographic techniques.

FACTORS ENCOURAGING TECHNOLOGICAL INNOVATION

It is not surprising to find special librarians as leaders in technological innovation and experimentation. Innovation is an entrepreneurial and risk-taking function, and special librarians, far more than other librarians, tend to exhibit this characteristic. However, there are other forces for innovation that reflect the environment in which special libraries are found.

Access to Computers in the Parent Organization

Many special libraries are located in organizations that began to acquire computers in the 1950s and 1960s for the mechanization of accounting and similar functions, including payroll, personnel and inventory. These machines excelled in the processing of large quantities of information for which relatively few and unsophisticated analyses were required.

The characteristics of these business files match to a remarkable degree those found in libraries, particularly for the control and housekeeping functions that so dominate many special library activities. Ordering, processing, announcing, lending and recalling are processes that center on relatively routine functions for a simple record which, once created, rarely changes. The normal library record includes author, title and classification number, and these three information tags are carried through virtually all transactions. Subject headings, the names of borrowers or the date of expected return may be added, but there is little complexity beyond this.

Initially, computers purchased by the organization for accounting, personnel and inventory functions were not fully used. It was therefore natural that managers of computer facilities would search for additional applications. Special libraries provided a very logical extension and thus became early users of automated equipment.

Small Collections

Special library collections are frequently small and specialized. They were therefore ideal candidates for the Termatrex and Uniterm applications in semiautomatic or manual systems, which worked best with document collections of 10,000 items or less. Further, once computerization became available, special library technical processes could be automated rapidly and at relatively little cost—certainly as compared to those of major academic libraries.

Unique Materials

As already noted, special libraries contain much material not already cataloged or analyzed by other organizations. While other libraries could purchase catalog cards, special librarians had to do their own cataloging. Expected or assumed workload reductions through the application of equipment were therefore seen as very real economies.

Self-imposed Standards

The willingness of entrepreneurs to innovate and take risks for a presumed reward has already been mentioned. Beyond this, however, special libraries tend not to have a commitment to a status quo for its own sake. There is no need, or at least there certainly was none during early stages of automation, to meet standards imposed by an outside library body or to expose decisions to the scrunity or approval of other librarians.

Freedom from Management Restraints

Special libraries are not particularly susceptible to overall organizational policies that might inhibit change. The indifference of higher management, which becomes a problem during budget negotiations, becomes an asset when changes considered minor by these upper-level administrators are contemplated. The library manager may well be told: "Do whatever you think best, as long as it doesn't cost any more." Restrictive as this authority may be, it nevertheless far exceeds the options available to many academic librarians. Special libraries are not run by their users, because the users don't care that much. Where library committees exist, they are usually advisory and rarely entrusted with policy authority, primarily because such an action would muddy lines of organizational responsibility and control.

In general, the elimination of library users from the implementation decision process is an advantage, because users tend to be more conservative and resistant to change than the librarians who are so often suspected of such characteristics. Resistance to change is frequently the result of lack of information. Special library users, who know little about what the library does and who have little expectation of improved service, cannot be expected to press for technological innovation. Where such pressure comes, it comes most appropriately from within the library staff.

Space Limitations

Because space problems are severe in many special libraries, the application of computer technology may be a particularly attractive option. This is especially true when such technology combines computer processing with microform output, as in the development of COM (computer output microform) equipment. Not surprisingly, special libraries were actively involved in the use of microfilms, microcards and microfiche as early as the 1920s and 1930s, long before computerization became feasible. These processes became particularly attractive in the 1970s and 1980s when it was possible to combine computer and microform technology.

Staff Limitations

The use of computerized equipment for repetitive library housekeeping operations is, at least potentially, a labor-saving device. It may or may not result in cost savings. However, even if automation produces no economies—and sometimes even if it actually *increases* costs—management is usually more willing to expend funds on equipment than on salaries. This preference is related to the peculiarities of organizational accounting practices, which will be discussed in Chapter 8.

MICROFORMS

For all the above reasons, special libraries have been well ahead of other types of libraries in the consideration of mechanical innovations and uncommon techniques. This characteristic was particularly evident in the early use of microform technology, undoubtedly prompted in large part by concerns about the adequacy of space. Reprographics, especially the use of microforms—which has now largely been subsumed in a larger category of computerized information technology—formed the prime thrust of activity in the 1930s and 1940s. It was the principal rallying point for the formation of the American Documentation Institute in 1937. It was only in 1952 that this society amended its bylaws to include individuals interested in other devices for literature storage and information retrieval; in 1968 it became the American Society for Information Science.

Detailed descriptions of reprographic technology and microform use are beyond the scope of this book. Briefly, there are two types of microform in widespread use. Microfiche is most effective for technical reports, specifications, drawings and other documents of up to 100 pages. Microfilm is most heavily used by libraries for periodical volumes or other works containing many hundreds of pages.

Interested readers can find many works which deal with the development of reprographics from both a technological and philosophical standpoint. We will note here, however, that the use of microforms in libraries has, from the start, generated strong emotional reactions. For many years, and to some extent even to the present, negative reactions were based on poor quality of film and on expensive and poor quality reading equipment. Despite technical improvements, some of the negative emotional response remains. Paradoxically, this feeling is being offset by a growing clientele that values microforms, particularly microfiche, because of the ease and economy of reproduction. The introduction of portable readers permits users to have their own collection of documents rather than just notes on index cards.

Whatever the factors in the consideration of microforms, most special libraries select them not from choice, but from the fact that space, cost or availability considerations make other forms of acquisition or storage impractical or impossible. The question, "How do you like microforms?" therefore has little meaning without the corollary question, "As compared to what?" Compared to full-sized copy, most users still prefer the latter. Compared to nothing at all, microforms begin to appear far more attractive.

OTHER EARLY INNOVATIONS

Many of the early information pioneers who worked on the development of microform systems were also in the forefront of the development of other mechanical and semimechanical devices. Many of these did not really reach practical levels until the introduction of accounting machine card-sorting equipment in the 1950s and 1960s. It is important to recall that these developments in special libraries and other industrial information settings preceded by many years the recognition by the computer industry that its machines had something to offer to this activity. Detailed discussion of these developments is unnecessary here. Only a few will be singled out for brief mention.

Termatrex and Uniterm

Both the Termatrex system developed by Frederick Jonker and the Uniterm system of

Mortimer Taube operated on the premise of posting documents to subject headings rather than subject headings to documents. This technique, which avoided the necessity of creating new cards every time a new item entered the system and required additions only for creating a new subject heading, worked on the principle of coordinated searching. That is, subject headings were compared to determine which documents they held in common. For the Uniterm system this was initially accomplished by a manual comparison of cards. In the Termatrex system, document accession numbers were posted to a grid, and a light shining through overlapping holes indicated those documents that held common subject terms.

The reader may recognize these approaches as early examples of coordinated searching, on which the most basic computer search strategies (A + B) are based. However, these systems operated without computers, and some examples of Termatrex installations are still in existence.

There were, of course, shortcomings. Most significantly, all documents had to be assigned sequential accession numbers, and unless they were also filed under these numbers, a secondary lookup was required. However, technical reports are frequently filed by accession number, both for density of storage and because browsing (the primary reason for subject filing) is difficult for report literature in any case. There are also collection size limitations.

However, both systems had several advantages. As "quick and dirty" approaches they provided subject access to a body of literature that most academic or public libraries totally ignore. Perhaps most important, subject analysis could be undertaken by individuals with relatively little or no professional education or training. Given the staffing levels of many special libraries and information organizations, these were and still are important considerations.

KWIC Index

One further approach to document retrieval that needs to be mentioned is the KWIC (keyword in context) index developed by Hans Peter Luhn. This index is based on the words in the title and on the assumption that the title assigned by the author is indicative not only of content but also of importance. Luhn's KWIC index, and several later variations and modifications, present what is essentially a dictionary with each item in the collection "subject-filed" under each of its significant title words. As with Termatrex and Uniterm, the phrase "quick and dirty" comes to mind.

These approaches, which have now been largely replaced by more sophisticated computer tools, are an excellent example of what early innovators in the special library and information center field were able to accomplish in establishing subject access for a body of literature unique to special libraries. This would otherwise probably have not been analyzed at all or been relegated to vertical files as in many academic and public libraries. It is also important to note that in these instances the level of mechanization—and the need for automated equipment—was marginal. However, these primitive systems were the basis for the far more sophisticated approaches now possible with computerization.

EARLY COMPUTER APPLICATIONS

The application of computer techniques to special libraries, starting in the late 1950s and early 1960s, followed no clear pattern of careful planning and implementation. This was true because special libraries were not using equipment designed and developed for their own use. They were adapting to equipment already in the organization, usually acquired for other purposes. These were large computers on which library applications shared and sometimes competed for time. However, fortunately for libraries, equipment that serves the needs of accountants is also well suited to library applications. As already noted, library "housekeeping" activities involving repetitive use of the same bibliographic item for ordering, payment, announcement, the generation of catalog cards, circulation control and overdue notices follow criteria quite similar to those used for accounting and inventory control. Special librarians who are now beginning to develop such housekeeping systems would be well advised to bear in mind the fact that their applications are not particularly specialized, unique or complex.

The use of computers for subject retrieval presents far greater problems. Unfortunately, many of the early special librarians in this field were immediately drawn to this application without gaining experience with simpler tasks. In addition to structural and searching complexities, the use of computers for retrieval also presents serious problems of cost-effectiveness. A file must be developed before it can be searched, and many months of costs may be incurred before any benefits are reaped. Furthermore, searching on the early machines was a sequential process in which library priorities frequently competed unsuccessfully with those of writing payroll checks or completing production reports. It is fair to state that the early years of special library automation were a mixture of successes and failures.

The problem of waiting in line for access to the computer was largely solved for the special library field—not because it was a problem for special librarians but because it was a problem for others. Also, significant improvements were made in computer efficiency. The development of time sharing, by which many input/output devices access one central mainframe computer, was possible because central processing is much faster than either input or output. Time sharing, combined with the use of telephone and other communications devices to transmit computer messages, permitted the development of online searching as we see it at present. That is, special librarians no longer have the responsibility of creating their own individual data bases on large in-house machines, although for some internal files they may continue to do so. They now search data bases supplied either by their originators (e.g., Dow Jones News/Retrieval Service) or through such intermediaries as Dialog Information Services, Inc. This approach also permits a simplification of search strategies, since intermediaries have developed software to permit the searching of many different data bases through one search strategy.

The technology of time sharing also made possible the promulgation of widely used library bibliographic networks such as OCLC and the Research Libraries Information Network (RLIN). Both the National Library of Medicine and the National Aeronautics and Space Administration (NASA) were among the earliest of government information programs to decentralize searching functions by giving users access to massive collections with the aid of a terminal.

GROWTH OF ONLINE SEARCHING

Online searching has grown phenomenally in only a short time, and it is literally impossible to obtain estimates of this growth with any hope of validity. It has been reported that the number of online searches in 1983 probably surpassed 4 million and that 100,000 individuals now have as their prime responsibility the searching of data bases. The growth has been particularly great in special libraries, which are far more dependent on outside information sources because of their own relatively sparse collections.

Online searching is not cheap, particularly because it represents what in accounting is termed a linear cost. That is, costs increase in relation to volume, and without quantity discounts. Basically, a doubling of terminal searching will double costs, and special libraries, like other libraries, have found that search costs are difficult to estimate and to control. Special libraries (unlike some public libraries) have made no attempt to reduce or limit their access to online information sources. They would be very foolish to do so. Inevitably such action would simply force users to turn to other sources and vendors, rather than to the library, for their information needs. This may indeed be happening to public libraries.

Despite the current popularity of vendor-supplied online data base searching, there is clear evidence of change. As in the past, this change does not come in response to needs voiced by special librarians. Instead, it comes through opportunities provided by the computer industry, which special librarians are beginning to seize. This new development is the evolution of smaller computers, especially microcomputers.

MICROCOMPUTERS IN THE LIBRARY

To some extent, the nomenclature is misleading, because today's micros and mini-computers have greater capacity than the "large" computers on which library processing began in the 1950s and 1960s. Microcomputers give the special library a processing capability under its own control, since the equipment normally does not need to be shared with another group. With completely free access comes a better ability to control and monitor costs as well. Most microcomputers are purchased rather than rented, and, once acquired, they are of course completely paid for. Furthermore, some special librarians find that the cost of such acquisitions may come from a central capital equipment budget, rather than from their own.

The most immediate use for microcomputers is for the internal housekeeping functions described earlier. Because microcomputers are not only excellent access devices but can also be coupled to rapid high-quality printers, they permit the special library to serve users at distant locations, something that has always been a problem. The special library or information center may now bring its internal file for subject searching back under its own control. Alternatively, it may undertake current awareness (SDI) searches from much smaller files on its own computers and leave the larger retrospective searches on the parent organization's large computer. (It is a safe bet that the latter computer installation is also undergoing changes.)

Finally, the special librarian may decide to bring at least some of the frequently searched outside vendor files into the library's own computer installation through a process called "downloading." The copyright and cost implications are not yet clear as data base owners grope for acceptable strategies. However, it seems clear that once a capability exists and individuals find it useful, it will be used. As with copyright adaptation to the development of dry xerographic copiers, data base vendors, like the rest of us, will have to adapt to what technology allows us to do and to the capabilities we want to utilize.

What results is by no means an either/or scenario. Special librarians will rely to some extent on all three options—microcomputers, internal mainframes and minicomputers, and vendor-controlled data bases. What combination is appropriate depends on the unique situation, needs and resources that each special librarian faces.

NEED FOR PERSPECTIVE

When considering the use of computers in libraries, it is important to place into perspective the many promises and opportunities constantly dangled in front of the special librarian. This occurs in the marketing presentations of hardware and software manufacturers and increasingly in the library literature by exponents who can sometimes exaggerate the impact of technology even as early opponents derided it as "nothing new or beneficial."

To a considerable extent the use of technology is simply subsumed within traditional library functions and operations, although not always with beneficial or effective results. As an example, the application of technology to the extensive and complex web of cataloging rules and conventions has undoubtedly done a great deal of good in facilitating exchange of data and avoiding duplication. At the same time, it could be argued that the existence of technology permitted a reexamination of the rules themselves, not just their transfer to computers. This should have been done because the premise of present-day cataloging rules is still based on the card catalog and its strengths and limitations.

The foregoing is intended as a caution to those who forecast sweeping changes in organizational structure because of technology. Although these predictions may be appropriate from the narrow standpoint of the technologist, individuals tend rather to make innovations fit to their own preferences and preconceptions.

With all of these cautions and caveats, it is nevertheless clear that computerization has had—and will continue to have—tremendous impact on the way libraries operate, on the products and services they provide, and on the way in which they interact with their clientele. This is true because, as already mentioned, special libraries are less bureaucratically structured and therefore more open to change. Also, special libraries, which are usually small organisms dependent on cooperation and resource sharing, are among the direct beneficiaries of the egalitarianism that computerization tends to bring about. That is, a library with only 20,000 volumes but direct access to millions more in bibliographic format and document delivery is now far closer in quality of collection to the research library which has several million books under its own roof. Only its method of payment differs. The research library pays for ownership (though this will gradually change); the special library pays for access.

THE LIBRARY MANAGER'S ROLE

The potential of automation for providing access to information materials outside the special library's own collection is clear. Taking full advantage of this capability requires a combination of terminals with which to search and access to software with which to undertake the process. Selection of computer hardware is in many organizations a centralized responsibility of the computer services department. Standardization is considered desirable from the standpoints of both price and maintenance.

While special library and information center managers cannot and should not ignore such overall policy directions, they must nevertheless assure that the equipment selected will be adequate, if not optimal, to meet their library's objectives and needs. This places on the special librarian the immediate requirement for spelling out what is to be accomplished, within what time frames and to what service specifications.

Special librarians are increasingly required to deal with specialists who have little understanding of the library's needs and who in turn speak about details that the librarian may not understand. The greater this tendency (and it will probably increase), the greater the need for the special librarian to spell out clearly and directly the needs that must be met. By definition, a computer system that does not meet those needs is unacceptable and should never be accepted for the sake of expediency or organizational consistency.

Establishing objectives has never been easy for librarians in general and is no simpler for special librarians. Most of them lack formal educational preparation in such skills, and users and managers expect little if any forward planning except in terms of budgetary controls. It is therefore important that special librarians maintain at all times a "wish list" of what they would like to have accomplished. They should show that list to internal experts and consultants with technological expertise. It is also important that they and members of their staffs participate, on a continuing basis, in professional seminars and reviews of the current literature to determine what may be possible and what their colleagues are doing.

STAFF TRAINING

The emphasis on technology and its potential does impose requirements on the special library staff, both professionals and clerks. Those requirements are less in terms of duplicating the hardware expertise and programming skills of the specialists whom, increasingly, the parent organization will house. Rather, they involve understanding both the advantages and the limitations of proposed options, as well as the ability to reconcile these to the program objectives of the library.

As an additional minimum, all staff members should be trained in the use of the

equipment made available to the library. At least some staff members should have sufficient understanding to be able to write program "patches," to make minor modifications
and to undertake preliminary troubleshooting. Increasingly, schools of library and information science are offering both courses and continuing education seminars on using computers, and professional societies are providing similar opportunities. It should be a clear
part of the special library's program plans and budget to utilize these opportunities.

Continuing education through specialized courses, workshops, seminars and even
degree programs will be necessary because the individuals now available as junior professionals are not likely to have already acquired many of these skills. A number of educational programs are increasing their hands-on emphasis on computer technology and are
exposing their students to the emerging options in access and delivery systems. However, a
substantial number, perhaps a majority, of new special librarians will continue to emerge
from undergraduate backgrounds in the humanities and social sciences. This will not be
because of any lack of recruitment effort, but because competition for science or computer
graduates will continue to be severe, with many opportunities providing greater immediate
financial rewards than librarianship.

EVALUATING THE IMPACT OF TECHNOLOGY

It is therefore crucial for special library and information center managers to take stock
of what changes an increased emphasis on computerization makes possible and desirable.
Much as special librarians have a great deal to learn about the appropriate application of
new technology, vendors and systems designers have even more to learn about the unique
characteristics of special library and information center applications. They are unlikely to
learn it, because they think their systems have universal application. One of the primary
reasons for a historical overview at the start of this chapter was to stress the point that,
while technology changes, problems in its implementation largely remain similar if not the
same. Some of the emphases and priorities that special library managers must consider in
the evaluation of technology are outlined below.

Equal Access to Information

There is no doubt that computer technology will provide a far greater "egalitarian"
access to needed information. In the past, ownership was the important criterion, but this
is no longer the case. The development of data bases accessible to anyone with a terminal,
a telephone and an electric outlet means that at least bibliographic access will be available
even to the smallest and most geographically isolated special library. It will also be available directly to that library's users, if they choose to avail themselves of that option. This
ramification will be discussed later in this chapter.

Document Delivery

The rapid expansion of bibliographic access capabilities has spotlighted the woeful
inadequacy of delivery systems. Largely still tied to the concept of cooperative interlibrary
loan as an exchange of favors, the present library delivery systems deal in weeks and
months—in comparison to a bibliographic access which is virtually instantaneous. Slowly

and almost grudgingly, bibliographic utilities are beginning to take responsibility for providing document delivery alternatives. The opportunities here are virtually limitless, but they are tied to realistic funding mechanisms. The delivery of documents has a cost, and its efficient delivery will have a price that exceeds cost, to offer an incentive to the provider. It will do little good to complain, as some academicians in small colleges have done, that this development thwarts their access to information largely collected in other institutions.

Whether these delivery mechanisms are funded by the requestor or subsidized by some other source is ultimately immaterial. The benefits are so substantial and the gap between bibliographic access and document delivery capability so great that a funding mechanism will most certainly be developed. In this regard, special librarians are already well ahead of their colleagues in the academic and public library sectors. Special librarians have been paying for document delivery systems for some time, including the practice of a two-tiered interlibrary loan charge, which makes such costs greater for libraries in the for-profit sector.

The cost of delivery systems will most certainly be substantial. It is simply another indication of the truism that it is not mechanization itself that is particularly expensive, but the ripple effects. Automation also raises expectations, and these expectations must be addressed, sometimes at an entirely new level of funding. As previously discussed, the level of special library funding is not really a central concern, because library expenditures are trivial as compared to the overall whole. The cost of enhanced delivery systems will have to be justified, but in all probability that justification will be far simpler than that of an additional cataloger or file clerk, because the benefits will be far more visible.

Options for Formatting Documents

The special library will have available to it a variety of formatting options for the delivery, use and storage of delivered material. It is already possible to transmit and store informational material in digitized form, and there is no reason to avoid doing this if the results promise efficiency and economy. Suggestions that information will be *used*, particularly by the special library client, in other than full copy form, are speculative and probably exaggerated.

Earlier portions of this chapter noted the negative reaction to the use of microforms by the library user, except when no other alternative exists. There is little doubt that users still prefer, and will probably continue to prefer, documents in full-sized hard copy. They now undertake online searches but ask for an offline printed product for delivery the next morning. While the special librarian may be required by organizational limitations to issue ground rules for what may or may not be produced in full-sized copy from either digitized or micro format, he or she would be very unwise to become the protagonist in this struggle. There can be a vast difference between what organizations dictate and what users prefer.

Arguments in favor of the "paperless society" ignore the fact that computers are superb, rapid high-quality printers. Anyone who is the regular recipient of information generated by computer (this writer, for example, receives daily student registration statistics for the entire campus) is well aware of the fact that the advent of computers has increased quantities of paper, not decreased them. This is largely because users still prefer the security of full-sized copy. Although time may modify this, it is not a change likely to come either rapidly or suddenly, and it will not have its beginning in the special library setting.

Similarly, suggestions for electronic journals as replacements for, rather than as additions to, printed copies ignore the pleasure and status which full-sized copies bring to both the author and the reader. Certainly for the academicians who are responsible for much scholarly publishing filed in special libraries, the microchip is not as yet an appropriate mechanism for transmitting of claims of scholarship to promotion and tenure committees. Publication-on-demand carries with it the threat that nobody will demand it, and this is a risk that most authors will seek to avoid if they can.

This is not to suggest that special libraries will not receive or store information in a digitized or microprint format. Such approaches may include videotext and video disc, not yet widely used in special or other libraries, but nevertheless with some potential for transmittal and storage. Experiments currently under way at the Library of Congress and the National Library of Medicine may make the applications of video disc technology even more relevant in the future.

The special librarian must in any case continue to be prepared to furnish a full copy at the request of the patron and would be foolish to turn that issue into a battleground. In fact, conversion of information from one format to another is rapidly becoming so simple and inexpensive that special librarians will be able to provide individual users with personal copies in a preferred format for retention or ultimate discard.

Handling "Marginal" Information

Enhanced technology will provide the special library the ability to manipulate "marginal" information, particularly from internal sources. The word is placed in quotation marks because in many cases such files contain the most important and most current information. Traditional library analytical approaches have concentrated on book material through mechanisms developed by the profession and on periodical articles as analyzed primarily by professional societies.

As noted in earlier chapters, special librarians have been in the forefront in developing techniques for capturing and analyzing what has been termed the fugitive literature. Early development of title indexes has been described in this chapter. These are now enhanced by full-text searching systems of particular importance in the legal field. These in turn are facilitated by that fact that, increasingly, the initial capture of data and the initial draft of the document are done on a computer. To the extent to which natural language search techniques can be and are being amplified, the raw material from which information search files are created is already in existence.

Historic concerns of special libraries about what to keep and what to discard, in the fear that unneeded material both competed for space and made bibliographic access more difficult, will no longer apply. Document storage can be compacted since enlargement on demand is simple. Bibliographic information storage on computers is also simplified, since additional memory is easily obtained. The emphasis will be on the training of skilled searchers and the development of effective search strategies. This will without doubt be the area of greatest contribution for tomorrow's special librarians and information specialists. This issue will be discussed below.

New Products and Services

We have known for some time that computers provide opportunities for products and services not available in any manual system. For these applications, direct cost comparisons are not possible, and estimates of user need and performance satisfaction must be developed. Two broad-scale examples will probably suffice; the reader's imagination can certainly add others.

First, special libraries with scattered user populations or collections diffused in branches can, for the first time, provide the "luckless" clients in overseas posts, marketing offices or isolated production facilities with equal bibliographic access and document delivery of required materials. Whether that delivery is across the hall or halfway across the world becomes immaterial. Wise special library managers can use this as a telling argument for the greater efficiency that comes with centralization of staff or collections or at least as an argument against the further splintering into minute local collections that users instinctively prefer.

The second example of the computer's potential to provide a service for which there is no manual equivalent results from the computer's ability to sort and interfile. This permits the compilation of cumulative indexes on a continuing basis. This writer first became impressed with this capability as director of the NASA Scientific and Technical Information Facility. Semimonthly published indexes to the NASA literature were prepared, and an annual cumulation, which included the December 15 index, was available by January 15 of the succeeding year. Almost all special librarians have had direct exposure to multi-year cumulations which, without computer capability, would have been too slow and expensive to compile.

While that technology is not new, it has been underapplied in libraries and will become particularly significant as the available data bases reach immense proportions. This will increase the requirement for specialized indexes, publications, bibliographies and reading lists, all of which can be pulled from the file in a variety of output formats. They can be transmitted electronically, via satellite, or via mail or messenger, and can be reformatted on receipt. The phrase "library without walls," which has been used to describe outreach services through the use of bookmobiles and traveling specialists, takes on entirely new dimensions under the described scenario.

SPECIALIZED DATA BASES AND LIBRARY SERVICES

The increasing development of specialized data bases, both in bibliographic form and in numeric or full-text formats, provides both opportunities and challenges for the special library manager. There are essentially two directions in which to go. They are not mutually exclusive, and in all probability a combination of both will be employed.

In-house Expertise

The special library will develop a greater in-house staff expertise. The traditional mix of one or two clerks for each professional may change drastically as clerical functions are mechanized and new professional duties appear. It need not be emphasized that this does not in itself provide cost savings. It probably increases costs. However, the greater emphasis on professional personnel and professional activities should contribute greatly to the increased status and visibility of the library.

The great profusion of specialized data bases and information services (the numbers change so rapidly that no accurate count can even be attempted) will increase the requirement for individuals with specialized knowledge and specialized training—training which, as in medicine, is never at an end. Some of these individuals will require advanced subject degrees. A number of the more forward-looking programs in library and information science are emphasizing dual degree programs. Some staff members may not require library or information science education at all, because the specialization of their work will emphasize exclusively advanced subject knowledge, perhaps at the doctorate level. Such a skill mix is not at all inconsistent with the standards for special libraries developed many years ago. It continues to be important to recognize and emphasize that these individuals are members of the professional staff and work under the guidance and supervision of the information center manager.

In some organizations it has been customary for technical groups to appoint information professionals as "gatekeepers," who interact with the information center on behalf of their colleagues. In general, this development is counterproductive, both because it tends to diffuse the authority and responsibility of the information organization and because it lengthens the communication chain. We know from many experiments that the more individuals involved in the transmittal of a request or a response, the greater the possibility for misunderstanding or error. Channeling the request through another professional is better than channeling it through a secretary, but it is best for the library to deal with each user on a direct basis.

Contract Information Services

The special library or information center manager can delegate, through contract or purchase, a portion of literature access to outside organizations that interpret information services and provide specialized searches and indexes. The use of contract and purchased services is discussed in more detail in Chapters 11 and 12. It will suffice at this point to repeat that headcount ceiling controls in many organizations housing special libraries are so overriding that it is generally preferable to purchase from the outside that which is available for purchase.

There is already a profusion of contract information services available, and the number will grow. These services perform duties ranging from routine searches and document delivery to complex analytical tasks that truly qualify as information analysis. These result not only in answers to questions but also in interpretations of what those answers mean to the specific objectives and programs of the parent organization. The special library manager should consider the employment of such specialized services as appropriate, but only under the control of the internal information organization.

The selection of these vendors, the letting of contracts and the acceptance of products must always remain under direct control of the information center or library. Any mechanism that permits technical groups to contract directly for computerized information work—and, paradoxically most important, that permits them to pay for it—will undermine the uniqueness and importance of the special library's contribution to the organization.

END-USER SEARCHING

A great deal has been written about whether the future will bring a greater development of intermediate information services or whether the future lies in the direct linkage between users and data bases, with special librarians facing an uncertain future or no future at all. Nobody knows precisely what will occur, but the predicted self-sufficiency of end-users is undoubtedly greatly exaggerated.

The argument is not new. As early as the 1960s, Project INTREX (at the Massachusetts Institute of Technology), the National Library of Medicine and the NASA information program were designing their online systems for use by end-users, be they aeronautical engineers or physicians. The attractiveness of urging such a scenario is not difficult to understand. Government information programs that claim to serve scientists or business executives appear more important and deserving of funding than those that serve "mere" librarians. The approach also has several other natural allies. These include the manufacturers of hardware and the developers of software, for the very same reason. They also include the developers and packagers of online search services, who would prefer a broader market, particularly one with perhaps less financial constraint or purchasing acumen.

The tidal wave of end-user searching that has been promised for the last 20 years has yet to engulf us. Most online searches of scientific and business data bases are still carried out by librarians and information specialists. This will probably continue, but it does not mean that there will be a total absence of end-user searching. The predicted profusion of terminals in every office and home suggests otherwise. Certainly end-user searching will increase dramatically if librarians make access to intermediary services cumbersome, time-consuming or annoying. Special librarians presumably will not harbor such a death wish.

Individual user searching will increase to some extent because of the efforts of data base producers and packagers to produce "user-friendly" data bases and search systems. Vendors of scientific and technical data bases, and also business, legal and general information files such as Dow Jones, LEXIS and *The New York Times Index*, have made strong efforts to reach users directly. They wish to impress these users with the capability and versatility of their products and to provide them with search software that is easy to learn and apply.

Other information services, such as The Source and CompuServe, are aimed at general consumers. It is still too early to evaluate the impact of these efforts, but this author remains skeptical. Perhaps it is because he recalls the glowing predictions for the use of home microfiche files to store recipes, an idea that has sunk into merciful oblivion. A greater reason for doubt is the fact that the developers of these systems believe that individuals, and particularly busy executives, like to sit at terminals and search. Despite all of the advertising, there is some evidence that this is not true. There may be confusion between using terminals for work and for playing video games. Even for the latter, there is substantial indication that the bloom is already off the rose. The suggestion that video journalism will destroy the local newspaper is also highly doubtful.

Individuals will of course continue to use computers and undoubtedly increase that use for work they have always done or wanted to do. They will also use computers for information access they have wanted and could not otherwise have. At the same time, a number of psychological studies have reported that executives consider the use of terminals for intensive work to be a clerical task and that they prefer to delegate such duties if they can do so with confidence. Enter the special librarian, who recognizes the professional potential of these activities.

In all probability, what will result will be a mixture of both increased end-user searching and increased access through intermediaries such as special librarians—but not necessarily special librarians, if we are not careful. The tremendous growth in all areas of searching should certainly provide opportunities for all protagonists.

Special librarians should offer training in online searching to users who want or ask to be trained. There is no doubt that some users will choose this option. They may be either those who really enjoy working at a terminal even after the novelty has worn off or, more likely, those who have never trusted the library to understand their individual needs and questions. There is no moral issue here, and librarians should willingly provide this service where it is requested. However, it would be a suicidal strategy to insist on providing such training or to decide that users should undertake their own work because it relieves the library of budgetary pressures by transferring these to user groups or because it lessens the library's workload or backlog. Some academic libraries have indeed adopted such a course of action. However, special librarians should continue to be guided by the recognition that their greatest contribution comes in doing work which others either can't do at all or can't do as well.

In general, special librarians and other trained information intermediaries will perform better and more useful information searches. This is particularly true for those searches that require inquiry across a variety of data bases, in different formats and through different search strategies. While the development of user-friendly systems promises relatively simple search strategies, such approaches are not only simple but also frequently simplistic. The reader should bear in mind the lessons of elementary mathematics. Common denominators are very useful, but they tend to be small numbers.

CONCLUSION

The impact of technology on special library and information center services is difficult to predict. We know that change is continuous, and the developments of the last 20 years have far outstripped our ability to forecast them. The changes to come will not be developed with special library and information center needs in mind, any more than they have been in the past. It is therefore important that we adopt changes because they suit our own needs, and not simply because they are available. It is equally important that we not stand on the sidelines waiting for a better system. A better system is most assuredly coming, but when it arrives, there will be a yet better one over the horizon. Managers waiting for the ultimate system will wait forever.

Even with all of these uncertainties, there are some things we can state with assurance. The first and most obvious is that tomorrow's special libraries will look different from today's. They will use more and different equipment of greater complexity and probably greater cost; they will produce different products and services of greater sophistication and specialization and with greater responsiveness; and they will require a different and more professional mix of staff. However, their mission will not have changed, except to grow in scope, in significance and in overall contribution. At least, that will occur if special librarians manage technological change and don't allow it to manage them.

We can predict with some certainty a continuing growth in total information sources, a growth in their complexity and a growth in the need for interdependent access to a variety of sources to meet information search requirements. Managing this process while giving the end-user better, but certainly not more, total information must be the primary objective. Overall, information services will most certainly be better. They will almost certainly not be cheaper, but they will most assuredly be more cost-effective.

SUGGESTED ADDITIONAL READINGS

Becker, Joseph. "How to Integrate and Manage New Technology in the Library." *Special Libraries* 74:1-6 (January 1983).

Boss, Richard W. *The Library Manager's Guide to Automation, 2nd Edition*. White Plains, NY: Knowledge Industry Publications, Inc., 1984.

DeGennaro, Richard. "Library Automation: Changing Patterns and New Directions." *Library Journal* 101:175-183 (January 1, 1976).

Epstein, H. "Technology of Libraries and Information Networks." *Journal of the American Society for Information Science* 31:425-437 (November 1980).

Grosch, Audrey N. *Minicomputers in Libraries, 1981-82: The Era of Distributed Systems*. White Plains, NY: Knowledge Industry Publications, Inc., 1982.

Jonker, Frederick. "The Termatrex Inverted 'Punched Card' System." *American Documentation* 11:305-315 (October 1960).

Kaske, Neal K. and Nancy Sanders. "Networking and the Electronic Library." *Library Quarterly* 17:65-76 (Fall 1981).

Kilgour, Frederick G. "Computer-Based Systems, a New Dimension to Library Cooperation." *College & Research Libraries* 34:137-143 (March 1973).

Luhn, Hans Peter. "Keyword-in-Context Index for Technical Literature." *American Documentation* 11:288-295 (October 1960).

Park, Margaret K. "Computer-Based Bibliographic Retrieval Services: The View from the Center." *Special Libraries* 64:187-192 (April 1973).

Pratt, Allan D. "Use of Microcomputers in Libraries." *Journal of Library Automation* 13:7-17 (March 1980).

Shaughnessy, Thomas W. "Technology and the Structure of Libraries." *Libri* 32:149-155 (June 1982).

Special Libraries Association. "Information Technology and Special Libraries." *Special Libraries* 72: entire issue (April 1981).

Taube, Mortimer. *"Computers and Common Sense: The Myth of Thinking Machines*. New York: Columbia University Press, 1961.

White, Herbert S. "Mechanized Information Processing and the Librarian." *Canadian Library* 19:64-69 (September 1962).

Williams, Martha E. "Criteria for Evaluation and Selection of Data Bases and Data Base Services." *Special Libraries* 66:561-569 (December 1975).

8

The Budget Process

Virtually all special libraries operate under the constraint and guidance of budgets. Organizations use budgets as a last line of control. While other techniques are normally employed to determine goals and achievements, the budget determines how much will be spent, even if what is going to be accomplished with the money remains unclear. In most management settings, budget preparation follows discussions of what is supposed to happen. However, as already mentioned, such planning discussions rarely occur between the library manager and upper management; communication about the budget is just about the only level of communication that takes place. As will be seen, that is a disastrous basis for any sort of decision process.

LIBRARIES WITHOUT BUDGETS

Some special libraries operate without a budget—an even worse situation. Managements develop budgets to control units that are worth controlling. The absence of any budget at all usually means either that the levels of expenditure are so trivial as to be considered under the heading of "petty cash" or that the librarian is not considered sufficiently competent to entrust with a budget.

Most of the budgetless libraries known to this writer do indeed have financial targets, but the librarian does not know what they are. Usually the librarian is asked to submit for his or her boss' approval whatever is needed. Then the supervisor approves or disapproves, based either on some sort of instinctive judgment or on a quick comparison with a departmental budget locked in a file drawer. A few special librarians even brag that their requests under this system have never been disapproved, which proves only that their own expectations are even lower than those established by management. Those librarians unfortunate enough to operate with a budget kept under the supervisor's lock and key must at least find out what the limits of that budget are, by making requests until some are denied and then trying to determine why they were rejected.

This author knows of only two special libraries in which the absence of a budget means that the librarian can really buy what he or she thinks is important, without further approval. In both instances the library administrator has been with the organization for many years and has developed a level of rapport and trust that assures management its confidence will not be misplaced. There are undoubtedly a few other examples of this situation, but it is so rare that no attempt will be made to explore it. Special librarians without budgets who can really spend what they like can skip the rest of this chapter. The more than 99% of the others either operate under budgets or should be attempting to wrest some knowledge of their budgets from their own management. Being underfunded is bad; being patronized or trivialized is far worse.

BUDGET BASICS

Some organizations make a great mystery out of their budget process, and some librarians insist they do not understand it. The procedure is really quite simple, particularly in the for-profit sector or in other organizations such as professional societies and foundations that must earn their income. The budget is a projection of income and expenditure brought into balance.

For organizations that sell goods or services, income can at best be estimated. It is risky to estimate on the high side because, in the final analysis, income cannot be controlled. Professional societies can estimate from past experience how many individuals will join or how many publications will be purchased, but if those targets are not achieved, there is really no recourse for increasing income. It is safer and certainly more prudent to concentrate on costs, which are projections about which the organization can do something. Increasing an assumed income to make it match desired expenditures can lead to bankruptcies, for organizations in both the for-profit and the not-for-profit sectors.

For institutions that receive their funds from one designated source, the budget process could be simpler, but it frequently isn't. Federal and state agencies would presumably know how much they had to spend if their authorizations were enacted before the start of the fiscal year. Universities may know what the legislature will provide and what student tuition will be, but not how many students will show up to pay it. In the for-profit sector, of course, the guessing game becomes most severe. Some of the factors that determine income are controllable; some are not. For example, changes in the interest rate affect mortgages, which affect housing starts, which affect the pulp and paper industry. Thus, although any budget process must include income projections, it can be clearly seen why concentration on costs is the more useful exercise.

For institutions that produce a product or provide a service in return for payment, there are costs directly connected to the income provided. If more cars or cans of beer are bought, more steel and more aluminum must be purchased by the manufacturer, and more employees must staff the assembly lines. Those costs may be greater than anticipated, but they are "happy" costs. Since they relate directly to the fulfillment of the organization's ultimate objective—the provision of a product or service and the return of a profit—these are called direct costs. In most organizations the cost of sales is also considered to be in the direct category.

The subtraction of direct costs from total income produces what is called a gross profit. By and large, all of the income has now been shown. (For the sake of simplicity, tax credits and interest income are not considered here, because the introduction of accountants' cash flow mechanisms is beyond the need for understanding of library and information center managers.) All further expenditures, such as rent, office supplies, etc., are called indirect costs. These expenditures reduce the profit already achieved and turn it into a much smaller net profit, sometimes even a net loss.

The use of the word "profit" should not be misleading. Organizations in the not-for-profit realm are obviously forbidden its use. They call their profits "surpluses," and the budget process is exactly the same. Even organizations that presumably have the mission to spend all of their money every year, such as government agencies, like to have a little something in reserve, to be used for contingencies and special year-end acquisitions. Some special librarians are told at year-end that there is money available if they can figure out how to spend it within the next five days. Experienced librarians have their plans for such largesse already in place: If they first have to think about what they will buy when the funds are offered, it is already much too late. Such special librarians never take vacation during the last two weeks of the fiscal year (usually in either late December or late June). Some academic libraries buy the majority of their books with year-end leftover money. It is a poorly designed process because it does not encourage careful planning and it cannot be depended on, but librarians must deal realistically with its existence.

INDIRECT EXPENDITURES AND THE OVERHEAD BUDGET

Indirect expenditures are not looked on with a great deal of favor and enthusiasm, particularly by those directly responsible for income and profitability. There is no tangible connection between these expenditures and what the organization does. The natural tendency is to keep them as small as possible, particularly because nobody really knows how large they should be. It has been mentioned before, but must be stressed again, that many of the decisions in the mahogany-paneled executive suites are made with pitifully little information in hand. This is particularly true in consideration of the indirect budget, also called the overhead or general and applied (G&A) budget.

At the same time, these indirect and overhead expenditures represent a significant part of the organizational fabric. Obviously, the organization cannot get along without its overhead activities, which include accounting, purchasing, personnel management, research and development, and administrative services. Further, some of these activities are managed by the politically powerful, including, for example, the chief executive's staff.

Organizational libraries and information centers are almost invariably housed in departments of research and development or in administrative services. That is, not only are these libraries themselves overhead organizations, but they are housed in an overhead cluster. The prestigious Director of Research or Director of Administrative Services is thus only a recipient of the organizational decision about the overhead budget, not the decision maker. The authority of this individual is usually limited to a determination of how the pie will be cut, not the size of the pie itself. That, of course, is important, but the librarian's leverage at this stage is quite constricted, because asking his or her boss to give the library a larger slice of the pie is asking in effect that some other subordinate receive less. Those individuals, of course, are also asking for more, with the implication that this be at the library's expense.

To understand how the game of bloodily carving up the overhead budget is played, usually to the library's disadvantage, we need only look at what happens in municipal budgets. Here expenditures are determined by income from taxes, and most municipalities are forbidden to spend more than they have. When allocations are initially made the library receives its share, usually far less than it needs or requested. However, when the police department objects to its assigned share and predicts dire consequences if it is ignored, the pie is recut and the library's share made still smaller. Since it still is the same size pie, it may not matter to the taxpayer. Of course, the library has the right to suggest that the police budget be reduced to provide more funds for bookmobile services, but such an attempt realistically has no chance of success.

WINNING SUPPORT FROM UPPER MANAGEMENT

The procedure for special libraries is similar in nature, although in this case the almost automatic disaster that befalls public libraries can be avoided, especially if the librarian has already cultivated the attention of senior executives. As noted, budgetary discussions provide little if any opportunity for members of overhead organizations to discuss programs and ideas. If these presentations have not already been made, it is now far too late.

The organizations represented in the overhead budget serve a very disparate group of functions. How does executive management evaluate the relationship between efficient purchasing, up-to-date accounting procedures, a pleasant and nutritious cafeteria, support for a new research project that may or may not pan out, a dependable internal mail and delivery service—and an efficient library or information center? It doesn't, because it can't.

It contents itself rather with a determination of the total level of overhead expenditures. This is expressed in dollars but is calculated as a percentage of the direct budget, usually either of direct cost or of income. It is, of course, an abdication of the decision process, but these are detailed decisions, which top management cannot make. And so it makes the larger decision of how much money is going to be spent, which is invariably far less than was requested, and then lets the subordinate administrators carve up the budget without any further interaction—unless there are specific activities that these executives really do care about. In that case, there are further instructions and guidelines on how the money is to be spent. Such "favorites" rarely include libraries, but they certainly can. Finding our protectors among those who determine the level of funding becomes the most effective strategy, and failure to do this can create sudden and terrible problems at times of budgetary pressure.

Not all times are times of budgetary crises, of course. There are periods of growth and expansion, and there are times when things pretty well continue as in the past. However, during none of these periods is support for overhead activities increased with any sense of gracious willingness by those charged with making the decision. There is no profit or surplus so large that someone wouldn't rather have it larger.

During times of financial stress, real panic can set in, and drastic steps are taken. It does little good to point out that an organizational recession is the worst of times to cut library support, because information needs will never be greater than during a period of searching for new options. The argument is valid, but it is also irrelevant, because management's responsibilities are, in the final analysis, measured not in the long term, but in the short term. The withholding of dividends accompanied by the promise of large dividends in five years will fail to impress a stockholder who hasn't even decided whether to keep the stock that long.

BUDGET CATEGORIES

Budgets are invariably put together and displayed in what is called a line item format. This represents the expenditure lines as they are carried in the organization's computerized accounting system. Budgets are presented in this form because of ease of display and of manipulation. It is certainly not because this type of arrangement conveys any information about how the money will further organizational objectives; it doesn't.

Although specific budget formats vary, we will treat three discrete categories as they affect libraries. The first is the labor budget, which includes the salaries paid to individual employees, perhaps broken into groupings but ultimately stated as one line for each employee, to accord with payroll records. For most special libraries the labor budget represents by far the largest category of expenditure, normally 60% or more. It is the largest category, and it is at the same time the least manipulable, for a variety of reasons which we will come to presently.

The second category, the library materials budget, represents the acquisition of books and journals. These should be only those for the library and not for retention in individual offices. The materials budget sometimes includes, and really should include, the cost of interlibrary loan and of data base searching, because these are alternatives to materials purchase. While the emphasis varies, a reasonable estimate for this category would be 30% of the budget.

The third group, frequently labeled for obvious reasons as "all other," accounts for the remaining 10% of the budget. Here we find such expenditures as telephone, travel, photocopying and postage. In the true validation of Parkinson's Law, which postulates an inverse relationship between attention and importance, this smallest of categories usually draws the greatest amount of organizational fire, not only for libraries but for other departments as well.

The Labor Budget

The labor budget may be large, but it allows few options. It represents individuals already on the payroll, and there is an understandable reluctance to terminate such people, for ethical, public relations and sometimes contractual or legal reasons. Moreover, the salary increases to be granted to these individuals may also have been predetermined and not left to lower management options. Few supervisors have the right, even if they chose to exercise it, to use money allocated for salary increases to enhance the travel budget instead. They may not even have the right to take salary increase dollars from one employee to give to another.

The ease with which changes to the labor budget can be displayed and totalled is the primary reason for the popularity of the line item budgeting approach. The alternative choices of 5% and 8% salary increases, or of 5% increases for clerks and 8% increases for professionals, can be factored quickly, and the budgetary impact can be calculated immediately. This is exactly how such decisions are made. The conclusions are reached first, and then the implementation mechanisms through the determination of percentages follow.

Firing individual staff members is of course possible and is sometimes done, but it is a tactic most organizations prefer to avoid. Salary cuts or the total absence of salary increases, are equally rare. The most convenient tactic for upper management to control the salary budget is to control the number of positions themselves. Quite simply, this means that new positions may not be created, and that existing positions are "frozen" as they are vacated by the incumbent. The process, called attritioning, is very much in vogue, because it avoids the need to make painful individual decisions and because it hurts no one individual. It is the process always used when government agencies seek to decrease staff and cost.

Attritioning may be humane for the individual employees involved in the process, but it totally lacks any form of direction and planning. Management gobbles up vacant positions as they arise. This can play havoc with the library's programs and plans, but the executives won't care unless convinced otherwise. As already stated, they are frequently not aware of any library programs or objectives except the quantitative measurement of repetitious activities, such as circulations or purchases of additional materials.

Staff reduction through attritioning also poses particular problems for the usually clerk-poor library and information center. Nationwide statistics indicate that clerical positions turn over at a rate three times as rapid as professional posts. In a rigid hiring freeze the library can quickly find itself without clerks, and even the departure of professionals will not necessarily coincide with the supervisor's priorities for the tasks to be performed.

Organizations frequently impose hiring freezes even in the absence of a budget crunch, because they recognize that hiring represents a long-term commitment, which is difficult to reverse. Hiring is considered a last resort, and understanding this will make clearer why some manufacturing plants prefer to schedule overtime rather than call back previously laid-off employees. Whatever the reasons or justifications, organizational constraints on hiring usually provide the greatest problem for the special librarian. Obviously, the special librarian must be prepared to select and hire if and when these restrictions are relaxed, and he or she must examine alternatives under which work can be accomplished through the expenditure of dollars rather than task assignment to staff members. Unlike many other organizations, special libraries frequently prefer to buy what they can and to do only what they must. This in turn creates the need to establish quality controls over performance in this environment—controls that are usually simpler to enforce when they involve library staff than when libraries must deal through the purchasing department, whose primary concern is cost, not performance.

The Materials Budget

The second category, the materials budget, is probably the least endangered, although there are always possibilities for cuts here as well. More likely, the materials budget will not grow as rapidly as needs dictate. A study conducted by the Indiana University Graduate Library School Research Center for the National Science Foundation, which was concluded in 1978, indicated that during much of the preceding 10 years the price of publications acquired in special libraries, particularly periodicals subscriptions, increased at a rate of about 14% each year. That would be bad enough, but we must also factor in the growth of the literature in a given field, estimated at anywhere from 2% to 8% annually, if we want to maintain collections of equivalent quality. Even using a conservative 3%, the library would require a materials budget increase of more than 17% each year just to maintain parity, and without allowing for expansion into new subject areas, which are bound to be needed in any special library. It is not surprising that special libraries are heavily dependent on other resources to supplement their collections and probably always will be.

Despite all of these concerns, the special library materials budget is probably the safest from the frontal attack of organizational budget cutters. This is true because cuts in the materials budget are most easily visible to the professional users, and management would rather alienate librarians than professional clientele. As already discussed, many individuals think of the library only as a collection, and the impact of cancelling a favorite subscription is quickly noted and draws a rapid response. As a basic strategy, special librarians should concentrate on protecting their other priorities, and let the users help in the fight for the materials budget. (They will, if you organize them toward that effort.)

There is only one caveat. As already noted, users find their way around limitations imposed by the library, in part by using their own funds. If the library materials acquisition program is curtailed by budget cuts, then the library must insist that departmental funds not be substituted. If that occurs, users will not notice the impact of reduced library materials and the library will lose its primacy and much of its importance. Further, no overall organizational savings will result.

"All Other"

The "all other" category, though representing a small percentage of the budget, is a favorite and continued target of budget cutters. In general, pressures on this category never end, even during good years. This is in part because "all other" is the only category in which budget cutters have freedom of options. Travel, for example, can be curtailed or stopped without affecting salaries or other benefits. The primary reason, in all candor, is the fact that management must create the appearance of economy at least as much as it must create actual economy.

OPTIONS WITHIN THE LINE ITEM BUDGET

The use of the line item budget in and of itself, without the invoking of plans and programs independent of the budget process, is truly disastrous for special libraries—as it is for virtually all overhead organizations. What options exist must be examined carefully. Several are suggested here; they will be discussed further in Chapter 12. If hiring freezes or headcount ceilings are in place, do they extend to temporary or part-time employees? In some organizations they do, in others not. Some librarians hire a good part of their staff for 90-day stints and have some employees who have worked under these conditions for several years. It is not, of course, a satisfactory arrangement and is certainly unfair to the people who acquire neither security nor benefits, but it is one approach when no other can be found.

When there is money but arbitrary constraints on how to spend it, the use of vendor organizations to perform services ranging from cataloging and pasting in pockets to bibliographic compilation is a possibility, provided that the library manager is free to choose and monitor the vendor and to make a replacement if necessary.

Similarly, computer costs can fall into a variety of categories. Hardware costs are sometimes handled through organization-wide capital equipment budgets, which do not penalize the library; for the library, therefore, purchase may be far preferable to rental. Computer line charges can be minimized in such an environment if the library or information center is able to place its own data bases on its own capitalized microcomputers or minicomputers.

What is important in all of these options is that the special librarian have control over both expenditure authorization and decision strategies. It must be remembered that, in any organization, the people who control the funds control the program.

PROGRAM BUDGETING: A BETTER APPROACH

Because of the obvious shortcomings of line item budgets in failing to provide either ranked alternatives or impact reports, the technique of program budgeting (often called PPBS, for Planning Programming Budget System) was developed more than 30 years ago, in large part by a management team at the Ford Motor Company headed by Robert McNamara. The PPBS approach still ends up in a line item budget; we still do what is convenient for accountants. However, that process is preceded by development of plans and programs, together with the resources necessary to carry out those programs, and it is from these decisions that line item budgets are constructed. If each of four programs requires a staff of two, then the staff of eight cannot be reduced without determining what program to curtail or eliminate. Conversely, staff is not increased without a clear indication of what additional work or service will result.

For libraries and other overhead organizations, the program budget approach is not a threat; it is their potential salvation. It allows the librarian to propose programs, and it then forces higher management to do its own job, something it is occasionally loath to do, particularly for overhead organizations. If programs are considered worthwhile, then they must be funded. If they are not funded, then those decision makers are clearly responsible for the choice, and it is their task to explain their rejection to disgruntled users.

Program budgeting places responsibility where it belongs, with those making the decisions. It is an absolutely essential process for special libraries. As already noted in earlier chapters, organizational executives have no guidelines concerning an appropriate level of library expenditure. They will spend as little as they can, and if that turns out to have no negative consequences, it not only validates the decision but suggests further cuts. Librarians have the unfortunate reputation of "somehow" making do even in the worst of situations. In some respects this reflects our service orientation, but it is not a characteristic that earns us either friends or support.

Despite a lot of organization propaganda to the contrary, it is not the responsibility of the special library manager to save the organization money. That doesn't mean that funds should be squandered, simply that the costs of worthwhile activities should not be a deterrent to requesting them, for several reasons. The librarian was hired to run a good library, just as the marketing vice president was hired to sell and the research and development manager to develop new products. Others, with more important titles and greater salaries, spend all of their waking hours and probably some of their sleeping hours guarding against the improper expenditure of funds. Let them do their jobs, and librarians theirs. Finally, even if the library manager were so inclined, he or she could not squander enough money to affect earnings by one cent per share in a corporate environment or to make a tangible difference in most not-for-profit organizations.

ZERO BASE BUDGETING

A discussion of budgeting requires a few words about the presently popular zero base budget. This is nothing more than a program budget that starts without the assumption of continuation at the present level. In principle, it requires revalidation of all ongoing activities, and it became fashionable when President Carter brought the concept to a very nervous Washington in 1977, although a significant article by Peter Pyhrr (listed at the end of this chapter) appeared years earlier.

In practice, zero base budgeting is not the threat it is made out to be. Despite wishful assumptions to the contrary, organizations have their own built-in bureaucracies, which are resistant to change. As one of the first candidates for a zero base budgeting exercise, the National Agricultural Library (now officially designated as the Technical Information Systems/National Agricultural Library) was asked to justify its existence in 1977. The task was not really all that formidable. The Department of Agriculture had built a brand new building several years earlier to house the Library. Does anyone really think there would be a willingness to agree that this was a mistake, and that the building should be converted to a silo? If librarians have plans and programs, they should be able to articulate these, even in the framework of zero base budgeting. If they have been too busy to think about plans and programs, they had better find the time.

CONCLUSION

Special librarians need to involve their own managers in the planning and decision process because in most situations librarians are too low in the organizational hierarchy to achieve acceptance of their decisions. They must recognize that these managers are also motivated by hope of reward and fear of punishment, particularly when they so frequently lack any clear idea of what they ought to do. Higher-level decision makers must be incorporated as clients to whom the library and information service has become useful if not essential. They will not support cuts if those cuts personally inconvenience them. They will still make cuts in overhead expenditures as originally planned, but they will direct them elsewhere.

One last injunction is in order. According to Peter Drucker, managers are given credit for only two accomplishments: innovation and marketing. Both of these ingredients must be present in the planning and programming process, and neither undermines the librarian's professional commitment to high quality service. It simply develops the support needed to provide that service. The next chapter will delve further into organizational political strategies needed for survival and growth.

SUGGESTED ADDITIONAL READINGS

Matarazzo, James M. *Closing the Corporate Library*. Op. cit.

Phyrr, Peter A. "Zero Base Budgeting." *Harvard Business Review* 48:111-121 (November-December 1970).

Randall, Gordon E. "Budgeting for a Company Library." *Special Libraries* 58:166-172 (March 1967).

Tudor, Dean. "The Special Library Budget." *Special Libraries* 63:517-527 (November 1972).

White, Herbert S. "Cost-Effective and Cost-Benefit Determinations in Special Libraries." *Special Libraries* 70:163-169 (April 1979).

9

Management Communication:
The Key to Growth and Survival

Some readers may feel a sense of vague discomfort at the emphasis on political and strategic tactics throughout this book. Librarians do not usually set out to be manipulators or wielders of power. They want to provide a service, the value of which they see as self-evident, and they expect others to be able to see it, too. This is particularly true of academic and public librarians. Most special librarians better understand the need to convince others of the library's value and to justify their requests for support. This requires a willingness to be innovative, assertive and visible, to insist on authority and to accept the responsibility that goes with such authority.

Librarians are often taken for granted, and they are often patronized; it is assumed that many of their requests are well-meaning and idealistic, but not practical. Librarians are not given credit for understanding the "real world" of organizational dynamics, and—to make it worse—they aren't expected to understand. The greatest danger for special libraries is the tolerance of special librarians who perform poorly, because the line between toleration and indifference is very thin.

Special librarians must insist that they be treated like all other managers, just as harshly and just as seriously. The term "manager" is used in a broad sense here, to describe individuals responsible for the management of resources. All special library directors must do this, even if they don't have additional staff as one of those resources. Special librarians must be able to demonstrate that they understand what is going on, that they realize when they are being given silly answers intended to be kind, and that they expect to be dealt with as professionals. In return, they plan to run their libraries effectively and responsibly, with resultant benefits for the organization.

THE LIBRARY'S COMPETITIVE EDGE

As an overhead service organization, the special library has several advantages over its competitors for allocated funds, because some of these other areas have very clear upper limitations. Once a corporate mail or cafeteria service becomes satisfactory, or even excellent, little can be proposed to improve it further. Mail service three times a day cannot be improved by providing it every 30 minutes. Once a cafeteria provides meals at reasonable prices and a pleasant atmosphere, it does not advance the organizational mission to add wine or strolling musicians. The librarian's ability to claim and propose improved information service is not so constrained, as long as he or she remembers to stress better, more accurate and more timely information service, and not greater quantities of documents.

DEALING WITH THE NEXT LEVEL OF MANAGEMENT

The library director must develop viable communications with his or her own management. This contact must be continuous, not simply restricted to those time periods when management wants to talk, which is usually when there is bad news about budget restrictions and other curtailments. Such communications cannot be avoided, but they must not be the only ones that occur.

The special library, of course, is not the only victim of these organizational communications problems. Many studies in personnel management have demonstrated that most of the flow of information is downward, with upper management informing lower levels of its decisions. Upward communication, in which not only needs but also ideas can be transmitted, is frequently discouraged, because the expression of unfilled needs is not welcome and because the transmittal of ideas is not expected.

Special librarians who wish to restrict their communications with their management to budget discussions can probably do so, particularly if the supervisor has no particular interest in the library and no expectation that the quality of service affects his own performance. However, as already emphasized in Chapter 8, this strategy is catastrophic in any organization, particularly for an overhead unit. Communication must be continuous, and it must concentrate on the development of ideas, plans and programs as a prelude to the budgetary discussions that inevitably follow. Administrators may seek to evade but cannot really refuse such approaches. Indeed, the library manager can take a more directly confrontational approach, pointing out to immediate supervisors that it is their job to help subordinates, that their duties include not only monitoring performance, but also assisting with planning and supporting initiatives when they are perceived to be correct. If they are incorrect, the librarian has the right to be told what is wrong with them.

ESTABLISHING GOALS AND OBJECTIVES

For the sake of simplicity this book will not discuss in detail the distinction between "goals" and "objectives," because these terms are used differently in particular organizations. Briefly, however, goals are usually considered long range, idealistic and unquantifiable, and objectives are specific, doable and measurable. It is important that objectives which are adopted be met, because a consistent failure to meet objectives or a tactic of revising objectives to match the "real world" trivializes the entire process.

The achievement of objectives in turn requires strategies. It is only at this point that the identification of needed resources comes into play. Goals without objectives are hot air, objectives without strategies are frustrating for the staff and meaningless for administrators. Things that are planned to be done should be done. If there is no thought of doing them, they shouldn't be articulated at all. If a change in circumstances forces prolonging or altering plans, then the implications of these actions must also be clearly understood.

Two other terms—"authority" and "responsibility"—must also be clarified in discussing objectives and the control of resources needed to achieve them. As these terms are normally used, authority is delegated to specific individuals (such as special librarians) so that they can accomplish stated objectives. Responsibility may be delegated in part, but ultimately must be retained by the appropriate level of management. If something fails to happen because of management action or inaction, then the responsibility must fall squarely at the feet of those who made the decision to act or not to act. There are elements of confrontationalism and risk in forcing management to face the issue of responsibility, and these tactics must be used carefully and prudently. In addition, the old story about the boy who cried "wolf" is applicable. If you threaten dire consequences unless support is forthcoming and that support is then withheld, you had better be able to produce the promised disaster or you will never be believed again.

Living with Reduced Resources

There are, of course, situations in which resources and support for the library will decline through no fault of the librarian or the immediate supervisor. This usually occurs when the larger organization has failed to achieve its own targeted objectives. Recent management literature contains the beginnings of discussion of management in environments with reduced resources. (Until about 10 years ago, it was generally assumed in management writings that all successful operations expanded and that, if an organization was not expanding, there was something wrong with its manager.) Librarians must understand this phenomenon, because at such times, despite the most eloquent justifications, budgetary reductions are inevitable.

Bo Hedberg, in a concise and interesting analysis of the problem of reduced resources, suggests that there are three stages through which an organization or a unit passes in the implementation of retrenchment. The first is to assume that the change is temporary, that nothing needs to be done because the problem will disappear. This is only occasionally true and should not be adopted as a tactic without specific evidence to justify it. Problems that are ignored do not disappear; they get worse.

The second stage is the assumption that the organization can continue as in the past, despite the reduction in resources, absorbing the additional workload by "working harder." This rarely, if ever, works. It clearly suggests that until then individuals were not working as hard as they could. The premise is both insulting and threatening, and individual workers will set out to prove it untrue even if perhaps it had some validity. There are other negative results as well, because this approach emphasizes quantities of work rather than the need to analyze what work actually should be done and how it should be done. The commonly heard complaint that individuals are so busy working that they don't have time to think about what they do becomes a terrible truth under these conditions.

Hedberg's third stage comes when it is realized that the change in resources inevitably forces a reassessment of objectives and strategies (or at least timetables) and may even require a redefinition of goals. Most simply put, it means that with fewer resources we do less, and the question is only one of deciding what we do less of. Obvious as it sounds, this is a recognition that organizations avoid as long as they can. Hedberg argues that it is only when the third stage is reached that the group really begins to come to grips with the problem; therefore it is desirable to move through stages one and two as rapidly as possible.

For manufacturing organizations, the relationship between reduced resources and producing less is obvious. No corporation can continue to make cars after it has sent home all of its assembly workers. For overhead operations, particularly for libraries, that connection is not as clear, and the assumption that libraries can do more and more with less and less exists because nobody has ever told administrators what can be done with what.

Thus, when facing reduced resources, the need for planning and the development of programs is greater than ever. It is essential to spell out what is presently happening, what ought to happen and what is needed to accomplish what ought to happen. The process is painful, because it requires a clear identification of what is now *not* happening. As will be shown later in this chapter, library reports usually concentrate on accomplishments rather than on unsolved problems, in part because management would rather not hear about problems and in part because speaking of accomplishments is more pleasant. However, the essence of meaningful management reporting is exception reporting. Supervisors want to know what went right, and there is no reason not to tell them. But, more importantly, they need to be told what went wrong and what didn't happen at all.

The tactic is risky, because there is always the option of beheading the messenger who brings the news of a lost battle, and management may be shocked to be told library service is bad. However, it is a risk that must be taken. To achieve progress, the difference between what is and what ought to be must be spelled out. Obviously, the administrators to whom these presentations are made have several options, including outright rejection or acceptance in principle with a partial or delayed implementation. However, the difference between the proposed target and the implementation plan must be clearly kept in sight, so that when questions arise about why certain things are not happening, the reasons and responsibilities will become obvious.

Innovation, the process of trying new and exciting things, is—perhaps surprisingly— particularly important during times of financial constraint, and another old management adage is worth remembering at this point: In organizational dynamics, it is usually easier to get a lot of money than to get a little bit of money. This is true because only decisions involving major commitments are worth an executive's time and attention and because the promise of innovation also provides the potential of credit for the administrator with the foresight to support that innovation.

The Library's Contribution to Organizational Goals

The special library's planned growth and improvement will ultimately be judged against overall organizational goals and objectives. The library's contribution to those goals must be claimed. This may be difficult to prove, but not difficult to demonstrate as reasonable.

Here we must distinguish among three terms frequently used in organizational evaluations—efficiency, effectiveness and cost benefit. Efficiency, as defined for the purposes of this book, means simply that whatever is being done is accomplished as quickly and cheaply as possible, whether or not the tasks are the "right" ones.

Effectiveness demonstrates the *value* of what is being done. The special library's value is in providing service to its users. The fact that most of these users are researchers, whose contribution to overall organization goals is just as indirect as the library's, can be a problem. Thus, it is advisable also to serve other users whose work is more directly productive and especially to serve all levels of management. Effectiveness is not difficult to demonstrate. Grateful users will usually help make the point, in agreeing that library assistance set them on the right track and saved them time. Such testimonials should be shamelessly solicited and passed along, particularly to convert those administrators who still consider the use of a library as an indication of weakness or uncertainty.

Effectiveness can also include cost effectiveness. For example, centralized purchasing by the library may be less expensive than individual purchases by separate offices. However, only if management is willing to give the library manager purchasing authority and to forbid others to buy the same material can the cost reduction be guaranteed.

Cost benefit—the "proven" reduction in other costs or the increase in income because of the effective presence of the special library—is difficult, if not impossible, to demonstrate. Although the library may point to specific instances when its activity saved time for various individuals, the library cannot determine what dollar difference that made. Similarly, while the head of the applied research group may readily acknowledge the support of the library, his enthusiasm will never extend to the willingness to reduce his own staff as a consequence. Fortunately, most administrators want to give at least the appearance of being reasonable people. If effectiveness is demonstrated and the opportunity for cost reduction and benefit is plausible, that is usually enough. It must always be remembered that the level of expenditure of which we are speaking is still minuscule compared to the total budget of the organization.

DISTRIBUTING OVERHEAD COSTS

In some organizations an attempt is made to distribute the cost of overhead services, such as the library, to its user groups. It is argued that in this way the organization achieves validation of the services, because presumably users are only willing to pay for what they consider worthwhile.

While the approach appears reasonable, it has definite drawbacks for the library. As just noted, the cost of library services is, for most organizations, a trivial expenditure. Breaking the costs down so that each department must, for example, justify the cost of an interlibrary loan becomes more of a nuisance than a control. In addition, as we know, users in almost all organizations have the opportunity to bypass the library, both for the purchase of materials and for the acquisition of special data base and bibliographic services. Little is accomplished in the implementation of a procedure if it is easily bypassed. Finally, the procedure of assigning overhead costs reduces much of the contact between the special library and its users to accounting transactions. Professionals may endure the need to deal with organizational accountants, but they don't enjoy the experience, and they don't consider it a professional interaction. A concentration on charging mechanisms undermines the relationship between fellow professionals which the special library works so hard to establish.

If a charging mechanism must be devised, there is a strategy by which the library manager can turn it to the library's advantage. Charging should be based, not on actual use, but on presumed use. In this approach an agreed-to formula identifying potential users is established, and the agreed-to library budget is allocated based on the number of professionals in each group being served. Since the purpose of allocation is accomplished and since the mechanism appears fair, accountants usually find this acceptable. In addition, it reduces the need for voluminous record keeping. More importantly, it places the emphasis on the use of the library as an earned benefit already paid for, rather than as an expense to be endured. It encourages individuals to use the library's services as much as they feel they need it. This approach can lead to increasing workload pressures and demands on special library services, but it should be abundantly clear at this stage that a disparity between needed and provided services is desirable in order for the library to grow. A problem must be created and made visible before it can be solved.

MANAGEMENT REPORTS

Management reporting tools have been mentioned briefly early in this chapter. In most organizations some level of official communication is prescribed, including certainly annual and usually monthly or even weekly reports. If specific formats are dictated, they must obviously be followed. However, if some options are provided, library managers should make careful and planned use of these, particularly if they know that these reports are forwarded to even higher levels of management or that they become a record on which further discussion, evaluation and planning are to be based.

The first point to be made about these reports concerns what to omit. In general, don't report what management neither understands nor cares about. Second, the report should be terse and easy to read. Executive summaries are very much in vogue. The use of graphs is helpful because it provides information at a glance and because it permits the writer to arrange the coordinates so that they visually emphasize the desired point. Fundamentally, a report should communicate both accomplishments and problems, usually accompanied by some sort of statistical summary to indicate level of activity. The statistics prove very little, but managers (like librarians) tend to be intrigued by numbers of items circulated, books received and reference questions answered. If these statistics suggest increased activity requiring additional support, then they can be very useful. However, the main thrust of the report must be the statement of accomplishments and problems.

Accomplishments should not reflect inwardly on the library, but on the contribution to the units being served. For example, the elimination of backlogs is important to management only in terms of what this does for or to library clients. Further, special librarians must be sufficiently astute to recognize that some user groups are more important than others in terms of their expected contribution to organizational sucess. If support for these groups can be spotlighted, it obviously should be.

Problems are more unpleasant to report, and management might even prefer not to hear about them at all, but they must be a part of the documented record. The special librarian should be prepared to propose a solution to the problem, if he or she has not already done so. If the problem is not then addressed, it must continue to be spotlighted. (As a special librarian this writer once had to comment on worsening space problems in more than 20 consecutive monthly reports. It was boring but necessary.)

Official reports are useful, and the librarian should not consider them a chore. We need to communicate because, without outside help, we don't have enough authority to do what we hope to do, and we get little chance to tell our story. A library restricted to annual reports, as some public libraries are, might as well not bother reporting at all. An annual report is a historic document to be filed, not a plan for action. Monthly and weekly reports are far more useful. Some of these require reporting against specific plans and programs, and that is excellent. Even if it is not required, the special librarian should incorporate that approach on his or her own initiative.

INFORMAL REPORTING METHODS

While formal reports are adequate tools for informing management about performance accomplishments and problems, they are poor mechanisms for the communication of ideas. The initial communication of new ideas should not be in writing if possible, particularly if the new idea represents a radical, controversial or expensive change. New ideas are threatening for most individuals; with very rare exceptions, people have an initial dislike for anything they find strange or different. Submitting new ideas in written form provides the reader ample opportunity not only to decide that he or she doesn't like them, but also to figure out why.

New ideas are best communicated through informal face-to-face conversations with your immediate supervisor. In this way, the ideas can be explored, sifted and modified, all without danger or risk, since nothing has been put on paper. Once the idea has been accepted, then it is time to propose it in writing, with the assurance that it will be approved at least at the first level of management, since it is only a confirmation of what has already been agreed on.

Informal meetings with management on a regular basis are essential. Staff meetings, in which much of the communication is downward, are not an adequate substitute. However, informal meetings are difficult to arrange. Managers will plead that they are busy; that means they are too busy for you and your problems, because they think they are dealing with more important issues. Informal meetings should occur at least once every two weeks, for a period of at least an hour. If one assumes a normal 40-hour work week, the reservation of one hour out of 80 for a direct subordinate is not unreasonable. In requesting such meetings, the special librarian must of course be flexible in agreeing to whatever time schedule suits the manager.

Given limited resources and an unlimited range of requests from subordinates, managers tend to establish the approval process as an obstacle course. Approval is made difficult, but it is assumed that competent managers will find a way. If they can't, then that is their bad luck. Further, it is recognized that competent and ambitious subordinates (and the two are frequently considered synonymous) will make demands on their managers' time, energy and resources. To put it most succinctly, managers commonly believe that strong subordinates cause a lot of trouble, but they are worth it. When the boss tells you in effect that he or she knows nothing about libraries, trusts you and expects very little contact, that is not a compliment. It is the ultimate insult. Supervisors save their attention for subordinate organizations whose performance matters.

Indeed, it is necessary to convince your superiors not only that the library is important, but that credit will accrue to them if you—and the library—do a good job. They already know they will get a certain amount of credit if they do nothing more than keep you within budget and avoid causing trouble at higher levels. Making them want to care is, therefore, a difficult problem. Of course, all managers can rationalize their performance as being in the best interests of the organization. Thus, it is not enough to argue that the library also serves those interests. Rather, you must base your approach on an understanding of the superior's personality. Some will care because they welcome an opportunity that will make them look good. Others prefer not to be noticed at all, and the only motivation that may work is one that causes them to understand that they will get into trouble *unless* they help you.

COMMUNICATING WITH LIBRARY USERS

No clear distinction between users and management is possible. Obviously, not all users are in the library's management chain, but all of the individuals in that management chain should be brought into the circle of users. In addition, other organizational decision makers should become users and supporters of library services. It stands to reason that since libraries are provided for the benefit of users, the opinions of these users will frequently be heeded by management more readily than the requests of the librarian.

Managing User Requests for Services

Because users are generally passive about the acceptance of information services, it is frequently necessary to encourage dissatisfaction by pointing out what services are not provided, or by indicating what is available to some users but not to others. However, the librarian must take care to direct user demands so that any new service does not offer convenience at the expense of quality. For example, users often request the establishment of satellite library locations for their convenience. Such requests should not be discouraged, but the librarian cannot afford to accept minimal installations that take the place of adequate library service. Users may simply accept poor service, blame the librarian for a lack of response or develop their own alternatives to the library, but inadequate service will not make them supporters of the library. The librarian must point out that satellite service has basic space requirements, and if these cannot be met, the service should not be offered.

Similarly, the service will require additional materials (frequently duplicates of materials at the central library), extra equipment and possibly additional personnel. Library collections cannot be serviced by secretaries in their "spare time" or by receptionists during slow periods. For one thing, it is dangerous for an employee to admit that his or her job does not require full-time attention. For another, the library will always be that employee's lowest priority. If part-time clerical assistance is to be assigned from another department, then the number of hours and the time frame must be specified.

Shock Tactics

It is sometimes difficult and painful to build a case for a stronger information service by pointing out the inadequacies of the present service. It may be a shock to clientele who felt that the library was pretty good, but it is a necessary shock. The easiest time to do this is when the manager is new (or when both the manager and the special librarian are new), so that there is no suggestion of personal accusation. It should also be recognized that for every new professional employee, and particularly those at management levels, there is a "honeymoon" period during which recommendations for major change are not only expected but treated warmly. That period may last only for six months, and it is necessary to move rapidly. It is also important to recognize that a manager or professional has a short attention span because his or her focus always shifts. The identification of a problem must be accompanied by at least a partial solution, the results of which can be quickly visible. In particular, increased funding support must produce tangible results within the same budget period.

Users can play an important role in helping to convince management to increase support for library service. Sometimes it is necessary to channel them into such a role through very direct irritations, although such an action involves risk. Nevertheless, at times there is no alternative. In one situation, for example, library space constraints had become totally intolerable for both the collection and the library staff. Repeated requests and justifications for more space had been ignored. As a last resort, the library director suggested the removal of all user tables and chairs, and their replacement by the needed additional shelves and filing cabinets. User reaction was instantaneous and voluble. Because the need had been demonstrated and documented so clearly in the past, additional space was provided in a matter of weeks.

The Library Advisory Committee

There are, of course, more positive methods of communicating with users and winning their support. Some of these were discussed in Chapter 6. Another is the development of a library advisory committee.

Such a committee should not make policy decisions or establish priorities for the library; this would be inappropriate and threatening to the librarian's management authority. However, an *advisory* committee, chaired by the special librarian and including a broad range of individuals who are sensitive to or can be educated to the need for a high level of information service, can be very useful.

An advisory committee serves three purposes. First, once the committee is informed about what the library or information center is doing and why certain policies have been promulgated, its members can pass on the information to their groups. This is particularly useful for explaining why certain restrictions are necessary. Second, the committee members can tell you what user groups need and want and what new priorities and directions are taking shape. If the library is going to provide anticipatory services, it obviously needs early information, and this is an excellent way to obtain it. Third, and perhaps most important, the committee can provide a broad and united front in communicating to higher authority what the library's needs are. Occasionally, these initiatives may come from within the user advisory group, but for the most part, competent special librarians should be able to anticipate unmet needs.

CONCLUSION

In summary, the development of a successful plan for insuring survival and growth rests on several general principles. In large part it must be based on an astute awareness of changing organizational initiatives and priorities, on support for projects that are considered crucial to success and growth, and on an understanding of what Peter Drucker has so clearly stated: In organizational dynamics, there are no neutrals. Individuals are for you or they are against you—because if they are not for you, they are for something or someone else.

The library manager must begin a careful process of engineered dissatisfaction, accompanied by reasonable and broadly supported plans for dealing with those dissatisfactions. This last is essential, given the short attention span of busy executives. The statement "never bring your boss a problem unless you also bring a proposed solution" is worth remembering.

As should now be abundantly clear, the greatest problem with management is not opposition but indifference. Special libraries must insure that they also serve the decision makers in the organization. This requires an understanding of who these people are, an attempt to orient both collection and services to their usually specialized needs, and a conscious plan to win over a group of people who are probably not instinctive or experienced library users. The dictum that individuals will support those services which they find personally useful holds for management as well, and management has the power to downgrade or eliminate services they do not use in order to provide greater support for those they do.

SUGGESTED ADDITIONAL READINGS

Bailey, Martha J. "Middle Managers Who Are Heads of Company Libraries/Information Services." *Special Libraries* 70:507-518 (December 1979).

Drucker, Peter F. Op. cit.

Echelman, Shirley. "Libraries Are Businesses Too!" *Special Libraries* 65:409-414 (October/November 1974).

Ferguson, Elizabeth. "The What, Why, How of Annual Reports." *Special Libraries* 47:203-206 (June 1956).

Hedberg, Bo, et al. "Camping on Seesaws: Prescriptions for a Self-Designing Organization." *Administrative Science Quarterly* 21(1):41-65 (March 1976).

Jackson, Eugene B. and Ruth L. Jackson. "Characterizing the Industrial Special Library Universe." *Journal of the American Society for Information Science* 31:208-214 (May 1980).

"Library Committees—Pro and Con." *Special Libraries* 50:235-243 (July/August 1959).

Park, Margaret K. "Decision-Making Processes for Information Managers." *Special Libraries* 72:307-318 (October 1981).

Special Libraries: A Guide for Management, Second Edition. Op. cit.

White, Herbert S. "Management: A Strategy for Change." *Canadian Library Journal* 35:329-339 (October 1978).

— — —. "Toward Professionalism." *Special Libraries* 60:69-73 (February 1969).

10

Technical Processing and Services

It has already been stressed in this book, as well as in numerous writings by other special librarians, that one of the most significant characteristics of the special library is its emphasis on immediacy. That emphasis includes an up-to-date collection, with a focus on ephemeral materials such as technical reports; rapidity in acquiring the materials and processing them for use; and speed in responding both to inquiries and to unexpressed but nevertheless very real needs. Much of what takes place in the internal workings of a special library deals with techniques developed to meet these premises.

BIBLIOGRAPHIC STANDARDS AND SPECIAL LIBRARY NEEDS

The library profession's ingenuity and skill in technical services has been concentrated on the descriptive cataloging or the establishment of bibliographic control over monographic material. This is largely because the Library of Congress, a major research institution with many millions of volumes and the primary force behind the cataloging process, analyzes material chiefly to meet its own needs for scholarship and accuracy. These standards, in turn, are particularly important for other major research and academic libraries. They are not nearly so important for most special libraries, where monographs form a relatively insignificant part of the collection.

Subject analysis is also aimed at broad general collections. Subject headings developed by the Library of Congress and others tend to be broad and general, partly because of the need to cover the universe and partly because, in order to be economically feasible, the system was designed to indicate the contents of a 1000-page book in at most two or three headings, which could be transferred to 3 x 5 catalog cards. The development of online catalogs has of course removed this economic limitation, but subject headings have not changed very much for two reasons. First, traditions die hard; second, it is difficult to effect change in such a massive organism with so much already invested in billions of existing cards. In addition, most libraries in the United States still do file cards and will continue to do so for the foreseeable future.

For most special libraries, the descriptive analysis of books by national bibliographic systems offers far more information than either the special libraries or their users care to know. On the other hand, the subject headings and classification numbers used by national systems do not have sufficient detail for the highly specialized collections of special libraries. This is not meant as a criticism of work undertaken at the Library of Congress or as reported through national cooperative systems. It is only intended to point out that these systems were developed for large general collections. Two brief examples from the Library of Congress List of Subject Headings will suffice. The subject heading "Shale Oils" is certainly adequate for a general library or even a special library in history. It is totally inadequate for a petroleum library where shale exploration may be a major organizational interest. Similarly, the heading "Marketing Surveys" conveys little in a library serving a market research organization.

CLASSIFICATION SYSTEMS

Classification systems cause similar difficulty, and special libraries have often found that the generally used systems, Dewey and Library of Congress, are far too specific for some parts of the collection and not nearly detailed enough for others. An aerospace or electronics library may find the Dewey classification more than adequate for the three art books in its collection, but will find the numerical breakdowns in its own fields of interest extremely lengthy and cumbersome, particularly when it is recognized that Melvil Dewey couldn't leave much room for disciplines that didn't even exist when he developed his classification structure. (The problem also exists in academic libraries when special collections are segregated for the benefit of their users. In the library of Indiana University's School of Library and Information Science, more than two thirds of the books in the collection are classified under the letter Z; some letters at the beginning of the alphabet are never used at all.)

In general, special libraries that still have an option will probably find the Library of Congress system preferable to Dewey. There are two very pragmatic reasons. The first is that LC will continue to be supported by the resources of the federal government and will provide the greatest opportunities for resource sharing. Since special libraries are staff-poor, they should acquire services whenever possible. Second, a classification system based initially on letters rather than numbers provides a greater flexibility with the same number of digits, and this becomes important when special libraries deal with books in their own area of specialization. There are 10 digits and 26 letters. Two numbers allow for 100 combinations, from 00 to 99. Two letters permit 676.

Some special libraries, occasionally in concert with others in the same field, have developed their own classification systems. Most have not, partly because most special libraries simply do not have that many books and don't normally classify their reports, and partly because the development of new classification systems is a laborious and expensive task.

HANDLING MONOGRAPHS

An increasing number of special libraries, recognizing their own staff shortages, have simply acquired cataloging information provided by LC or other sources and applied it uncritically. In these libraries, the task of cataloging—and particularly of descriptive cataloging, which is so important in academic and research libraries—is usually performed at the clerical level. (For some special libraries, of course, particularly those that serve a national research clientele, book analysis can be as important as in any major academic library.)

While most special libraries do not expend much effort on the analysis of book material, they nevertheless buy quite a few books. These volumes are sometimes for the library's own collection, sometimes for the retention of individual users and user groups. The importance of separating the latter transactions from the library budget has already been stressed. Nonetheless, it is probably advantageous for the special library to handle the purchasing transactions. Librarians know where to buy specific books; purchasing departments usually do not. Furthermore, libraries have access to discounts for volume purchase, and can make them available to the entire organization. The librarian should always make sure that such service is recognized and credit received. In fact, some special libraries even purchase personal copies for individuals through their book vendors, passing along to the organization's employees both the convenience and any discount received.

Special libraries must decide how much processing to do for books acquired for outside departments and individuals with organizational funds. As a minimum, some sort of accounting records are maintained, and a property stamp is affixed. These books are, after all, organizational property, to be returned if and when the recipient leaves the organization. It may also be desirable to establish some minimum bibliographic controls, particularly for those books that have been uniquely acquired for a particular department, which the library does not own at all. It is always possible that, at some future time, another employee will need access to one or more of these books.

Beyond this, not much processing is recommended. Detailed processing of materials that will be retained permanently by others is expensive and time consuming; it may also convey the misleading impression that these books are indeed available for library use and access. It is only a short step from this conclusion to the one which suggests that the library need not buy certain material at all, because it is already available.

Emphasis on speed of processing tends to dominate special library decisions in the area of technical services. There simply can be no excuse for delays of six months or longer, which are not uncommon in academic libraries. Once received, material—especially items requested for a particular user or project—should be available for use within two weeks at most. If the special library is unable to meet that sort of schedule, it may be better to let the user have access to the material first and to catalog it later. To deal with time pressures, often exacerbated by staff shortages, special libraries should consider simplifications in the ordering and cataloging processes, including the use of outside vendors.

Some vendors deliver books as ordered and, for a fee, deliver them cataloged and processed, with circulation records, spine labels and pockets already in place. Special libraries that use the ordering and cataloging processes as a continuing program to develop online records must keep their system requirements in mind and hold the selected vendor to rigidly developed procedures and formats. However, this can generally be accomplished.

PROCESSING PERIODICALS

Most special libraries do relatively little in-house analysis and processing of periodical articles (for many special libraries, the major source of current information) because the periodical literature is largely already indexed and analyzed by commercial services and professional societies. These organizations, with their many years of experience, tend to be detailed and specific in their analysis, using the terminology of the special library's clientele. It is important to remember that the users of special libraries feel no particular obligation to learn library terminology. Instead, the special library, as a service institution, must adapt its subject descriptors to the nomenclature of its users. These usages change frequently and rapidly, and generally the commercial and professional society services that undertake periodical indexing keep abreast of these fluctuations.

Use of the major indexing services also has one other immediate advantage: It expands access to information well beyond the holdings of the individual library, one of the major needs of special libraries. As already noted, indexes produced by professional societies and commercial organizations are increasingly available both in published form and through online computer access. The proper mix of what to buy and what to access cannot be generalized in this book; it depends very much on individual conditions. It can only be stated that it is important that the special librarian and information center manager adapt the service provided to the need and not make users fit preconceived service approaches.

PROCESSING NONTRADITIONAL MATERIALS

It is in its treatment of the so-called nontraditional literature—reports, pamphlets and brochures—that the special library really differs from its academic counterpart. Technical and business reports are not generally analyzed by the Library of Congress, nor are they processed through networks or cooperative services. While some are distributed through government agency programs and indexed by these organizations, others have a far more limited distribution. Some may be acquired specifically by only a few special libraries to meet a particular need. Some carry security restrictions. Finally, a large number are proprietary reports produced within the sponsoring organization itself and so are unknown outside that organization.

These items represent, for many special libraries, the most significant and useful portion of the collection. They are relatively brief; they deal with specific, narrow topics; they are informally produced; and they are likely to be of interest for a relatively short time. The development of techniques for handling literature of this type truly sets special libraries apart.

As has been noted, the general types of subject headings developed for national research collecti ns of monographs are not sufficiently detailed and specific to permit subject analysis of this literature. Some special libraries have in the past developed their own lists of subject headings (in some instances as a sensitive and proprietary publication because it tells a great deal about the organization's own research involvements). In some cases groups of special librarians, acting as a Special Libraries Association Division or as a nucleus group within a chapter, have developed subject term lists for specific subject disciplines.

Government agencies and professional societies have also developed lists of subject headings for specialized fields, and these have been used, adapted and modified. With the introduction of computerized search strategies, these subject heading lists have increasingly been replaced by thesauri, which permit searching of specific terms and of terms related through see-also references, and which allow a hierarchical development of search terms through which the search can be broadened or narrowed.

Indeed, the development of computer searching, now common in many types of libraries, was initially almost exclusively undertaken in special libraries and is still a far more active task in these settings. Computerized searching is a great deal more sophisticated than manual searching, which permits only one idea or term to be pursued at a time. Computerized searching permits the permutation of search terms and, in addition, eliminates the economic limitation imposed by the need to produce catalog cards. It is still not unusual for document indexing systems to operate at two levels—a manual system, which uses one set of terms for retrieval through card files, and a computer retrieval system, which includes these terms plus an additional set of analytical descriptors to provide greater depth.

The techniques discussed so far require a detailed analysis of each document by an individual familiar with both subject content and nomenclature. Even when such people are available, it is an expensive and time-consuming process for materials which may be of short-term interest. For this reason, special libraries were among the first to experiment with nonintellectual index approaches, taking advantage of clerical activities or other data capture already undertaken, to produce indexes usually referred to as "quick and dirty."

The most obvious example is the use of title indexes, based on the premise that titles for technical reports are usually fairly specific and informative. Titles can be manipulated through computer processing to produce keyword in context (KWIC) indexes or keyword out of context (KWOC) indexes, in which the entry word is displayed separately. Title indexes can be enriched by adding words or phrases not in the title, but this of course introduces both costs and delays. A more promising approach, made possible by economies of computer storage and the capture of information during the initial process of report generation, is to search on more than just the title—for example, abstracts and summaries, or even, particularly for legal documents, the entire text.

ADDITIONAL RESPONSIBILITIES

Special librarians are often asked to take on additional activities, perceived by organizational management as related to the processing of materials (at least, they don't know what else to do with these tasks). These activities most frequently include responsibility for a central file, records management or the organizational archives. Taking on these additional responsibilities is not unreasonable for the overall health of the library or information center, provided that additional staffing and resources are furnished so that the quality of service is not diluted. Additional tasks require additional resources, and organizational administrators know this. However, that won't stop them from at least trying to get something for nothing, if you are pliant enough to let them get away with it.

CONCLUSION

This brief chapter has described technical services and processes that are unique to special libraries. No attempt has been made at detailed discussion of the full range of technical services. As noted in the preface to this book, much of what occurs in special libraries is characteristic of all libraries. The author assumes that readers are familiar with basic, behind-the-scenes library procedures or that they can easily find information in numerous other works on the subject.

Technical services in special libraries differ because of the emphasis on nontraditional materials and on speed of information delivery. Another distinguishing feature of special libraries is their reliance on outside resources. This is the subject of Chapter 11.

SUGGESTED ADDITIONAL READINGS

Russell, Dolores E. "Records Management: An Introduction." *Special Libraries* 65:17-21 (January 1974).

Special Libraries: A Guide for Management, Second Edition. Op. cit.

11

The Library's Dependence on Support from Others

Special libraries recognized their need to cooperate from the very beginning. Their small size, the limitations of their collections and the uniqueness of some of their problems were all instrumental in the decision to band together in the Special Libraries Association. Once organized, special librarians immediately undertook cooperative activities designed to deal with very direct and specific problems.

The cooperative development of union lists, subject heading lists, catalogs and other helpful tools has characterized special librarianship. The development of two major indexes, the Public Affairs Information Service and what is now the Applied Science and Technology Index, was mentioned in Chapter 2. Special librarians began these indexes because they needed such tools to perform their work, and nobody else was producing them.

Similar cooperative ventures, too numerous to detail, have been developed by SLA through local or regional chapters, subject interest divisions or just as a loose confederation of members. For example, the Special Libraries Association, in cooperation with the John Crerar Library in Chicago, established a translations center so that expensively prepared translations in one library could be available to others. One of the Association's members, Frances Kaiser of the Georgia Institute of Technology Price Gilbert Library, spent virtually all of her free time over several years in the compilation of a directory of translators and translation services. Why? Because special librarians needed such a directory, and there was none. The Rio Grande Chapter of SLA, with many members who work mainly with government documents, developed a Dictionary of Report Series Codes for their own use and for that of other libraries with similar problems.

In addition to cooperation among colleagues, special libraries rely on a number of sources for support and services from both outside and within the parent organization. This chapter will discuss interlibrary loan, document delivery, government reports, the use of commercial services and consultants, and issues in dealing with other overhead departments within the organization.

INTERLIBRARY LOAN

Because of their normally small holdings and because of the esoteric interests and needs of many of their users, special libraries have always had a greater need to develop methods for acquiring materials from outside sources than have other libraries. Academic libraries, particularly major research libraries, have far greater holdings, in some cases millions of volumes, with which to serve the needs of research faculty members, and the needs of students can be easily predicted from syllabi and course outlines.

Borrowing versus Lending

Interlibrary loan as a cooperative system has always been based on the premise that it was a reversible transaction. That is, all libraries were both lenders and borrowers, so there was really no need to maintain records indicating who did the borrowing and who did the lending. That premise, attractive as it may seem, is based on a fallacy. While it is true that just about all libraries borrow, and that presumably as many would be willing to lend what they could, many statistical studies indicate clearly that there are "net" borrowers and "net" lenders. Net lenders are concentrated primarily in major academic libraries. Net borrowers include a great many small libraries and just about all special libraries.

Special libraries are borrowers rather than lenders for a number of reasons. Their small collections, including unusual and proprietary documents not listed in bibliographic tools, is one. Another is that special libraries rarely have multiple copies, and they feel a responsibility to keep heavily demanded material on tap for their own users. Finally, many special libraries are not open to the general public. Special librarians, who are part of a larger profession dedicated to a free and complete interchange of information, are sometimes forced to operate under constraints that make such interchange difficult or even impossible. They must accept and deal with that limitation.

Special libraries have traditionally preferred to borrow from other special libraries. There are several reasons for this. Borrowing from academic libraries is frequently slow, particularly as these libraries realize that good service only encourages more requests. Special libraries are usually willing to lend to each other in a much more informal environment, based on a telephone request and without the completion of the laborious documentation required by the American Library Association code. Special librarians, particularly in the same geographic area, tend to know one another, and it is always easier to ask a favor of a friend. Finally, in a lending-borrowing relationship between special libraries of equivalent size, a reasonable balance is possible.

However, special libraries must still borrow heavily from academic institutions. In return, they lend very little. Articulate and thoughtful special librarians have worried about this unbalanced relationship, about the perception of special libraries as "moochers," and some special librarians get very defensive and indignant at the implication that they don't pull their own weight.

The inclusion of more special library materials in network data bases has opened collections to access by other libraries. It has also been suggested that special libraries encourage the use of their collections and facilities by other libraries. This is hindered by the fact that many of the materials in a special library are proprietary and internal, and, as noted before, some organizations even consider their list of periodicals to be proprietary. Nevertheless, special libraries participating in state and regional networks have, in some cases for the first time, informed other libraries of their holdings.

Special Libraries and Library Networks

Special library participation in library networks has been neither immediate nor automatic. As networks and cooperatives were initially established, special libraries, especially those in the for-profit sector, were frequently excluded because of the fear that their participation might affect the consortium's tax-exempt status. Those fears have now largely disappeared, and special libraries do belong fully to networks and consortia, both those among special libraries and those of national and regional organizations that include all types of libraries. However, attempts to broaden special library participation in network lending activities are probably doomed to failure, because the unique characteristics of special libraries will tend to continue to make them net borrowers. Further, cooperative activities that place labor workload burdens on the special library are probably best avoided. As noted previously, the special library's scarcest resource is generally its supply of labor.

The Costs of Interlibrary Loan

By the late 1950s, academic libraries began to realize that interlibrary loan was an expensive activity and started to impose charges for lending material. Even though charges were limited to direct, out-of-pocket costs, they represented a significant expense to special libraries and other borrowers. State agencies have stepped in to subsidize the lending process within regional networks. The Medical Library Assistance Act carried a formal recognition that lenders incurred a cost for which they should be reimbursed, even if perhaps at a level considerably lower than a proper accounting cost. The word "perhaps" is used because no study to determine an acceptable accounting cost for interlibrary loan has ever been undertaken or considered politically acceptable. This writer suspects that the present cost, including the appropriate allocations for overhead costs, might be around $12 per transaction. The use of such numbers might change some conceptions about what should be bought instead of borrowed, particularly if an item is borrowed repeatedly. To some extent the continued subsidization of interlibrary lending creates a false economic picture. Some publishers have argued that it might sometimes be more appropriate to subsidize purchase rather than lending if subsidization is indeed appropriate.

However, these arguments may have little effect on special libraries. Some lender libraries, expressing resentment at borrowing by special libraries, particularly those from the for-profit sector, have established dual charging mechanisms under which these libraries pay a higher and presumably more realistic fee for the privilege of borrowing. These tactics are of dubious legal and moral validity. A publicly supported academic or public library is on shaky ground when it attempts to discriminate against a corporation that supports it through taxes. Even private universities cannot afford to antagonize those organizations to which they turn for support, scholarships and donations. Nevertheless, as far as this writer knows, these dual charging mechanisms have never been confronted or challenged by the special librarians who are their victims. It would be interesting to find out what happened if they were.

In any case, the special library's readiest contribution to the quid pro quo of interlibrary lending is money. Scarce as it frequently is, it is still the most easily acquired resource for special librarians, certainly as contrasted to obtaining space or people.

There are also alternatives to the separate and direct payment for each separate loan transaction. The most obvious involves the use of deposit accounts. Another, which has attractions for libraries as well as for their parent organizations, involves a generous, tax-deductible annual donation from the corporation to the academic library. In return, certain levels of information access, including borrowing, are provided. Special libraries that rely heavily on a local university can hire students on a part-time basis to copy material daily from the collection on public copying machines. This alternative is attractive for the special library because it provides daily turnaround. It is attractive for the student, particularly if the university has a library school and a future librarian is engaged. Finally, the procedure is attractive for the academic library, because academic libraries don't really enjoy lending, no matter what they charge. (There are legal issues involved in copying material, of course. These will be addressed later in this chapter, in the section on cooperating with the legal department.)

DOCUMENT DELIVERY

There is no doubt that the need for access to outside document collections is increasing. The development of data bases and online services has done a great deal to increase bibliographic access (the knowledge that material exists) without improving document access (being able to get a copy). It is easy to see that this can lead to frustrations for users and special librarians alike. Divulging to users only what is in the card catalog and therefore also in the library is a much simpler approach, but it is one which will never be available to us again.

A survey undertaken for the National Science Foundation (NSF) by the American Society for Information Science in 1975 indicated that the greatest concern among information professionals was not for the development of additional and more sophisticated techniques for bibliographic access, as the NSF had assumed. Instead, it was for the development of adequate document delivery mechanisms to support highly sophisticated bibliographic access systems already in place.

One generally available alternative used by a number of special libraries is the document service offered by commercial organizations, sometimes in conjunction with an online search. Partly in response to pressures and needs revealed in the NSF study and other investigations, data base vendors and packagers have taken a greater responsibility for providing copies of the documents indexed by their services. Usually these are periodical articles, and they may be provided directly or by arrangement with one of a number of reprint services. Use of these mechanisms has the advantage of speedy delivery; some services promise to fill all requests within 24 hours of receipt and to mail them via overnight delivery or courier if this is desired. Most of the time it is not, but there are exceptions.

The use of a commercial service also serves to bypass questions of copyright restriction, since the service will include in its charge whatever it has to pay the copyright owner. The most obvious disadvantage is the greater cost. For some special libraries, that may put documents out of reach. For others the cost may be unimportant.

GOVERNMENT REPORTS

Special libraries are heavy users of products and services produced by agencies of the federal government. For some libraries, particularly those in the defense industry, government reports may be the greatest source of current information. For a considerable time these documents, produced by such agencies as the Department of Defense, the Department of Agriculture, the National Aeronautics and Space Administration (NASA) and the Atomic Energy Commission (now the Energy Resources and Development Agency— ERDA), were provided free of charge or only at the nominal cost of reproduction and distribution. Starting in 1968, this policy has gradually changed. Government agencies are now expected to recover their costs, and both the Government Printing Office and the National Technical Information Service have been placed under stringent cost-recovery guidelines.

The wisdom of such decisions can be questioned, because the government spends many millions of dollars in support of research. It may appear foolish to refuse to spend any more to inform potential users of the research that has been undertaken. Nevertheless, these philosophies of cost recovery are in full sway and show little indication of change. In addition, the federal government in particular has embarked on a course of spinning many of its own former products and services off into the private sector.

This policy has contributed to the rapid development of the information industry and has had a drastic impact on the special libraries that purchase many government publications. For example, since 1966 the price of the *Bibliography of Agriculture*, first marketed directly by the Department of Agriculture through the Government Printing Office and then sold through a succession of commercial organizations, has increased from $6 to $345. Special librarians and information center managers should not be surprised at these changes; those located in the for-profit sector can hardly object to the transfer of publications from the public to the private sector. However, difficulties can arise when such arbitrary and sharp pricing changes are put into effect suddenly and without adequate prior notice—and after the library's own budget has already been submitted and approved.

SUPPORT FROM COMMERCIAL SERVICES

The development of commercial information services has been one of the phenomenal growth stories of the 1970s and 1980s. It is disturbing that some of these organizations were established, not to serve libraries, but to serve library users dissatisfied with the level of support and willing to pay for better response. Ironically, limiting the library's budget and thereby the levels of service it can provide may sometimes lead to greater expenditures outside the library budget. This phenomenon has already been described at length—being bypassed represents one of the greatest dangers for the special librarian. If at all possible, commercial information services should only be used when the library or information center manager has decided to use them.

Subscription Agents and Book Jobbers

One heavily used support service is that of a subscription agent for periodicals and of a jobber for the acquisition of monographs. Occasionally, both functions are provided by the same organization. Subscription agents and book jobbers usually serve special libraries in a variety of roles. From a purely clerical standpoint they consolidate purchase orders and invoices and permit greater clarity of accounting records. They also handle currency exchange for foreign subscriptions, and they act as intermediaries for claims and other correspondence. On a professional level, major subscription agents are far more familiar with publishing activity, particularly in obscure fields and overseas areas, than most special librarians can possibly be.

Book jobbers serve a similar function and are particularly valuable in the acquisition of overseas titles and in assuring that continuing volumes of a publications set are received. In addition to generalists for both periodicals and books, there are specialists who deal with specific disciplines or the foreign market. Out-of-print materials are handled by yet entirely different organizations.

Subscription and book agents are only as good as the reliability of their service, and their value rests in saving time and energy for the library staff. These qualities far outweigh questions of discounts or applied service charges, which vary from one service to another. These are frequently negotiable, and no library should pay more than it needs to. At the same time, the library manager cannot simply abdicate to the purchasing department the selection of the vendor, usually the lowest cost vendor, without a consideration of service quality.

Other Services

Other outside services available to the special library include those that provide both clerical and professional temporary personnel (by which one may bypass organizational manpower ceilings), those that can recatalog or reclassify an entire collection, those that undertake reference and bibliographic services, those that prepare microforms and indexes, and those that develop computer software.

Special libraries frequently find the service "make-or-buy" decision tilted toward purchase because of space or personnel limitations. Moreover, as Herbert Landau points out, there are instances in which specialized qualifications or economies of scale make outside purchase an attractive alternative. Specific decisions will vary with the preferences and options available to individual library managers. As will be discussed further in Chapter 12, it is generally preferable to contract clerical tasks and retain professional activities. When any functions or services are contracted, it is essential that the library manager retain control over the selection and retention of vendors, over the development of specifications and over the determination of whether work has been satisfactorily completed.

Contracting for All Library Services

The last several years have seen the contracting of special library functions brought to the ultimate degree, with the suggestion (particularly in the federal government) that the entire special library service should be provided by outside contractors. This writer regards these proposals with considerable apprehension, particularly when the contracting delegation is so complete that the organization does not retain a qualified special librarian or information scientist to supervise the work being undertaken.

There are two reasons for this concern. The first, already stated in earlier chapters, stems from the phenomenon of acceptance of low-level library services by their users, the inability to differentiate between the service that is provided and the service that should be provided. In the absence of professionally developed and monitored performance standards, both the contractor and the monitoring agency will inevitably look for shortcuts and economies, actions most likely at the expense of qualities of service.

The second reason stems from the recognition that in times of budgetary curtailment, contracted services are both the easiest and most politically attractive to cut, since they have no direct impact on any of the permanent staff to which the organization has legal or at least moral responsibilities. While the contracting of specific functions under the control of the special library manager is in many cases a desirable practice, the suggestion that the entire operation be contracted and all operational controls be removed is potentially disastrous.

USING CONSULTANTS

As with other acquired services, consultants may serve a very useful purpose, or they may waste time and money and also have a negative impact on staff morale. The most obvious and direct use of consultants is to provide an expertise that is not available within the organization and that will be required only for a limited period of time. Specialists in systems analysis, computer hardware selection, space planning, and the preparation of special reports and analyses are in this category. They should be selected carefully—good consultants are expensive; cheap ones are frequently not worth their cost. Consultants should be given carefully defined parameters of work but then also afforded considerable freedom of approach within those parameters.

Consultants can also be useful for overall evaluations and surveys of the efficiency and service levels of an information center organization, for comparisons with similar outside special libraries and for conducting user studies. Carefully selected consultants for such tasks, serving on a time-limited basis, can undertake work for which regular staff may have neither time nor training. They bring a level of objectivity to the task which is not possible for employees. Finally, and sometimes most importantly, the consultant can reach levels of upper management that the special librarian often has difficulty approaching. Organizational dynamics indicate that individuals who have been hired at considerable expense should be listened to. Consultants should only be employed when their judgment and opinion are genuinely desired. They should never be used simply to add credence to decisions already reached, terms under which most ethical consultants will not accept assignments.

COOPERATION WITH OTHER DEPARTMENTS

In addition to its dependence on services provided by organizations and individuals outside the parent body, the special library is also dependent on cooperation with and services from other groups in its own organization. The special library must be able to work successfully with these units, because they control resources and expertise not otherwise available to the library manager. Further, organizational rules demand consistency and adherence to standard procedures.

The relationship with the personnel department, of paramount importance, is explored in Chapter 12. Other departments with which the special library must work are computer systems, purchasing, accounting and legal. All of these groups are, like the library, overhead service organizations. They make no direct contribution to overall performance or profitability and have no purpose except to assist those who need their services. Like some special librarians, individuals in these areas may forget their own role and begin to act as though the organization existed to serve them. It is sometimes necessary in negotiations to stress that it is the other way around and to issue a few helpful reminders.

The Computer Systems Department

Special library interactions with computer operations and systems-support departments go back almost 30 years. Special librarians recognized early the ways in which computers could help overcome their unique problems of lack of staff, lack of space, lack of time and specialized collections not already cataloged by others. The lengthy history contains many superb accomplishments but also many tales of horror. Computer center managers, anxious to increase their own activities and thus to justify more staff and more elaborate hardware, frequently enticed librarians with offers of free computer access and free systems support. As the staff of systems analysts became busier and the computer time fully allocated, librarians began to understand how little priority they had when compared to either direct profit-producing operations or the accounting department, which controlled the machine. There were instances of computer searches which took only a few minutes to run, but for which computer access was provided only once a month.

Special librarians are still learning the lessons of these early experiences. Perhaps systems analysts or computer center managers promise more than they can deliver, or it may simply be that library activities are difficult to estimate. In any case, the special librarian must control the relationship with what is after all another service group, which has as little direct impact as the library (although normally computers have a good deal more visibility). Librarians must determine the specifications of computer systems designed for them—not necessarily in terms of detailed procedures, but in terms of the products and services to be produced as well as the time frame for these activities. If what is projected is not acceptable, it should be rejected.

It is usually a good idea to provide funds in the special library budget for both computer access and systems support, even if these funds are transferred in an internal accounting transaction. Controlling the budget provides at least the potential of spending these funds for outside service bureau operations, the threat of which is usually enough to improve the quality of service. In addition, microcomputers, as discussed in Chapter 7, provide an important opportunity for independence for the special librarian.

The Purchasing Department

Under normal circumstances special libraries have little need of the unique services of a purchasing department. Libraries usually know what they want to buy, what it costs, and from what organization they wish to make the purchase. The help of the purchasing department is usually required only for the acquisition of special supplies or equipment for which the library has a knowledge of neither vendors nor specifications. These situations are relatively rare.

The interposition of the purchasing department is, for the special library, frequently a nuisance and sometimes an expensive one. A particular problem arises when there is pressure to select a periodicals or monographic jobber purely on the basis of price, without any consideration of quality of service, dependability or rapidity. In such a situation, there is little alternative to confrontation between two overhead service organizations, each intent on carrying out what it sees as its job. That the special librarian is right in insisting on criteria besides cost matters little. It becomes essential in these situations for the librarian to put his or her own management to work, convincing them of the correctness of the library's position and insisting that they carry out their responsibility in fighting for a proper solution.

A second problem in dealing with the purchasing department can arise when this organization insists that all library purchases be placed through formal organizational purchase orders. The argument is usually that this is necessary for consistency and control. However, as we have noted in the case of the special library, procedures developed by and for the convenience of an overhead organization make little impression on higher management. Many of the things purchased by special libraries are inexpensive; some reprints cost less than a dollar, and even most special purchase books cost less than $100. Ideally, the special library should have the ability to initiate or request checks, as controlled by its own budget limitations, up to amounts of perhaps $500. It should also be able to establish deposit accounts with frequently used vendors who require prepayment, such as government agencies, and have accounts for the acquisition of interlibrary loan or photocopies.

Where all persuasion fails, a simple search of the literature of purchasing will disclose the organizational cost of placing and processing a purchase order. It will be difficult for any manager to defend a policy under which it is more expensive to maintain controls than to purchase what is being controlled. Most purchasing managers whom this writer has known and battled have helped search for a basis for compromise when confronted by the knowledge that their costly illogic would be appealed to higher levels of management.

The Accounting Department

Although accountants are frequently the dispensers of bad news regarding budget curtailments or expenditure disapprovals, they are not the policy makers who determine what the special librarian or information center manager will be allowed to spend. That decision is made at other and higher levels of management. Accountants only monitor performance against the targets which have been established. One of the reasons for working in close cooperation with accountants is that they are interested in control and in knowing not only the level but the purpose of expenditures. Much of the special librarian's energy must go toward establishing responsibility for and control over his or her financial commitments, and in this endeavor accountants can become natural allies. When librarians can point out to financial managers that the organization is controlling only the *library's* expenditures for information materials, while other groups' information expenditures are larger, uncontrolled and unspecified, they often strike a responsive chord. Establishing centralized control and responsibility in the library can be presented as an attractive proposal to the accounting department. It is true that some accounting functions establish procedures that are needlessly complex and restrictive. However, when this occurs it also affects other units in the organization, and the librarian's complaints won't be alone.

The Legal Department

If this book had been written before 1977, it probably would not have had to mention the relationship between special librarians and organizational attorneys. However, the 1977 revision of the copyright law does pose some legal concerns for special libraries, particularly those in the for-profit sector.

Publishers have become increasingly belligerent in pressing their claims and have established a Copyright Clearance Center to facilitate the collection and distribution of royalties for material that has been photocopied. Many librarians, including special librarians, have disputed publisher claims and urged the maintenance of a hard line. However, there have been relatively few cases. None have gone through a full process of litigation to the awarding of punitive damages, and most have been settled out of court, for several reasons. It is impractical for publishers to claim punitive damages from librarians, and it is not considered good publicity to sue academic institutions and other not-for-profit organizations perceived to operate in the public benefit.

If litigation does occur, it will probably involve special libraries in major corporations, which borrow and copy extensively. Because of this likelihood, most of the activity of the Copyright Clearance Center is with special libraries in the for-profit sector. It may not be worthwhile for corporate special libraries to maintain a confrontational attitude and risk the threat of litigation. Financial settlement may be preferred, particularly because the sums are usually fairly trivial for the sponsoring organization. (Obviously, if the decision is made to participate in the Clearance Center or some other copyright payment mechanism, the funds implementing this decision must be added to the library budget.)

In any case, special librarians would be well advised to avoid making such decisions unilaterally. In consulting organizational lawyers, however, it is important to bear one consideration firmly in mind. Attorneys are specialists with but a single function. It is their responsibility to protect the organization against legal entanglements and sometimes also against legal embarrassment. They have no responsibility for the successful or profitable operation of the organization itself and certainly none for whether or not the special library functions efficiently. Their charter is much narrower. Organizational attorneys tend to fall into two opposite categories. Some are highly belligerent and combative, anxious to stretch their interpretations of the law and to be able to prove in a court fight how good they are. Others are intent on avoiding confrontation at all costs and will always urge moderation and caution. Either way, their attitude has nothing to do with the problems of the library, although it may reflect the philosophy of the parent organization.

The librarian should think twice about seeking an organizational legal opinion. Once that opinion is presented, the library is stuck with it, even if it is framed as, "We're not sure, so don't do it." Moreover, as always in interpersonal relationships within a management framework, librarians should know something about the attitudes and philosophies of the attorney they are planning to consult. Failing to anticipate what the other person is likely to do or say is always dangerous, but particularly so in this case, because the advice of lawyers is invariably accepted by those who employ them.

CONCLUSION

It is one of the recurring themes of this book that the special library, to a much greater extent than other libraries, is not a self-sufficient organization. It depends heavily on services provided to it by outside vendors and by internal service units within the parent organization.

In dealing with outside groups, it is important that the special library manager retain control over the process of selecting services, of establishing criteria for qualitative standards and for time-responsiveness, and of replacing those vendors whose performance is unsatisfactory. Invariably, this depends on developing realistic expectations and financial arrangements and on retaining all management controls, particularly financial controls, within the library.

In addition to the acquisition of outside services, usually through purchase, the special library, especially one in a corporate environment, must also rely on services provided by the organization's other overhead and service groups. It is important to remember that these units are as dependent on the perceived value and benefit of their services as is the special library. They are, in many cases, just as vulnerable to organizational economy drives. The special library, as a user of these services, is as entitled to useful cooperation and support as are the library's potential users to its services.

SUGGESTED ADDITIONAL READINGS

Dagnese, Joseph M. "Cooperation between Academic and Special Libraries." *Special Libraries* 64:423-432 (October 1973).

Hamilton, Beth A. "Principles, Programs and Problems of a Metropolitan Multitype Library Cooperative." *Special Libraries* 67:19, 23-29 (January 1976).

Kaegbein, Paul and Renate Sindermann. "Cooperation among Special Libraries at the International Level." *Special Libraries* 72:390-398 (October 1981).

Kingman, Nancy M. and Carol Vantine. "The Special Librarian/Fee-Based Service Interface." *Special Libraries* 68:320-322 (September 1977).

Landau, Herbert B. "Contract Services in the Special Library: The Make or Buy Decision." *Special Libraries* 64:175-180 (April 1973).

Mason, Marilyn Gell. *The Federal Role in Library and Information Services*. White Plains, NY: Knowledge Industry Publications, Inc., 1983.

Murphy, Marcy. "Networking Practices and Priorities of Special and Academic Librarians: A Comparison." University of Illinois Graduate School of Library Science Occasional Paper No. 126, December 1976.

Robinson, Barbara M. "The Role of Special Libraries in the Emerging National Network." *Special Libraries* 72:8-17 (January 1981).

Sass, Samuel. "Must Special Libraries Be Parasites?" *Special Libraries* 50:149-154 (April 1959).

12

Professional and Clerical Staffing

As already noted in earlier chapters, special libraries and information centers have a great deal of difficulty in establishing and maintaining a proper mix between clerical and professional staff. Part of this problem stems from the failure to understand what a library *can* do and what a library *should* do.

The most highly visible activities in any library are clerical functions. These include the workings of the circulation desk, the filing of catalog cards, the shelving of materials and the demand for the return of overdue materials. Professional duties, such as the compilation of literature searches and the detailed analysis of material, are usually performed in a back room, out of view of the special library's users—if indeed they are performed at all. This phenomenon is most apparent in major academic libraries, where it is possible to encounter dozens of students and clerks in the transaction of daily activities without ever seeing a professional librarian. Since much of the special library's clientele have had their most recent exposure to library service in academic settings, it is not surprising that they bring these perceptions with them and assume that most of what librarians do involves clerical activity.

PROFESSIONAL QUALIFICATIONS

Added to this is the preference in almost all organizations, and particularly those in the for-profit sector, to provide promotional opportunities from within. If what a professional librarian does is neither visible nor understood, it is not surprising that personnel administrators see library "professional" posts as a promotional opportunity for loyal clerks. Emphases on internal promotion have increased over the last decade, in response to pressures of clerical unionization and affirmative action goals. A considerable portion of the clerical work force is female or belongs to minority groups, sometimes both. It is understandable that personnel administrators, who fail to appreciate the professional responsibilities of the task and who perceive this as a "female" profession, often see library positions as the potential solution to their own problems and the organization's commitments.

These concerns are not new, of course. Certainly they predate, and so cannot be blamed on, recent emphasis on either affirmative action or basic competency. In the mid-1950s, when this writer first entered the ranks of special librarianship, it was still an accepted practice for airplane manufacturers to appoint to the post of company librarian widows of pilots killed while testing experimental models. The argument was that, although this woman might not possess any tangible job skills, the corporation owed her a "white collar" post with some dignity and prestige, which she could perform without education or training. Why not appoint her librarian?! It is reassuring to recognize that, while we still have problems of professional identity, we have come a long way since then.

Education versus Experience

On the other hand, educational qualifications for professional posts in special libraries should be neither categorically arbitrary nor automatic. A later section of this chapter will examine the process of job descriptions and job evaluations, which ultimately determine the qualifications and skills required. The professional library degree represents neither an exclusive nor an automatic qualification, but it does represent the most direct and most effective path. It is certainly true that there are holders of accredited MLS degrees who function as clerks; some even appear to enjoy it. It is also true that some individuals whose only preparation is on-the-job training have performed superbly as professionals. Properly written job descriptions that concentrate on levels of performance can make allowance for both of these situations.

It is equally true, however, that there continues to be, throughout librarianship and particularly in special librarianship, pressure for the downgrading of professional preparation requirements. In some cases these are expressed by personnel administrators as equivalents between education and experience. As noted later in this chapter, this is a perfectly acceptable approach. However, it presupposes a clear understanding of the concepts and philosophies as well as the skills to be acquired during this process. Experience that measures only time and does not demonstrate continued growth shows little except perseverance. It is when personnel administrators fail to understand, and special librarians fail to demonstrate, the professional requirements of the post that the temptation to supplant librarians with clerks or to promote clerks to the status of librarian becomes particularly attractive. Once this occurs, the decision becomes self-validating. Given the organizational lack of understanding, what they do becomes what they are supposed to do.

Subject Expertise versus Library Expertise

In many special libraries, as well as in major academic libraries, there is yet another pressure that can result in the appointment of a nonlibrarian. This is the desire to seek subject as well as library expertise, sometimes by requiring a dual master's degree or even a subject doctorate. Some of the major schools of library education are making an effort to respond to this need by offering dual master's degree programs. However, some subject backgrounds are more plentiful than others among library students. The likelihood of finding one candidate suitably prepared in two disciplines is greater when, in addition to librarianship, we seek American history rather than petroleum geology.

There are no simple solutions to this need, and we have come to recognize the importance of continuing education to acquire knowledge and skill that cannot be imparted in the initial academic setting. This is true both because the library and information science profession continues to change and also because no academic program can anticipate totally what will be required in any particular position. Academic degree programs, particularly at the bachelor's and master's levels, still approach professional preparation through common denominators.

At least for some special library posts, the skills and perceptions imparted in library education may be more important than those developed in subject training. Such subject preparation is increasingly narrow, while the work of special libraries becomes increasingly interdisciplinary. An understanding of the library behavior patterns of scientists and engineers, a recognition of frequently employed literature formats and a knowledge of basic scientific tools and nomenclature would appear to be more important than a degree in a specific scientific discipline such as organic chemistry.

Library educators, like employers, appreciate the advantages of graduates with appropriate double preparations, and some progress has been made in reducing the imbalance between what is needed and what is available. It is important to stress in this chapter only the recognition that insistence on subject skills becomes yet another reason for the use of nonlibrarians in what are supposed to be professional library positions.

Professionals and Nonprofessional Duties

There is another side to this coin. Not only do clerks and nonlibrary professionals function as librarians, but professional librarians function as clerks. This is an even greater problem. As previously noted, there is a great deal of clerical and routine activity in any library and therefore in any special library or information center. The relative relationship of clerical to professional work will vary, depending on the type of literature used and the amount of labor-saving automation employed. It will also differ among structures emphasizing either centralization or decentralization of services. Branch libraries involve not only a duplication or scattering of material but also an additional need for staffing. Much of that staffing is concerned with the clerical routines of library housekeeping and control.

STAFFING RATIOS

Special Libraries: A Guide for Management suggests that there be at least one clerk for each professional, and this writer agrees with this as the minimum ratio. Thus, every special library including a professional must have a staff of at least two, with a clerk supporting the librarian. If only one individual is available, that person should probably be a clerk, because he or she will be functioning largely as a clerk. For larger libraries, the appropriate relationship of clerks to professionals maybe 2:1 or even 4:1.

There is no general rule of thumb for the ratio of clerical to professional staff, because no two special libraries function in the same way. The use of computers and of contract services can decrease clerical pressures, while a concentration on circulation and interlibrary borrowing or the development of branch collections will increase them. At a minimum, each special librarian should recognize the situation that confronts him or her. This can be done by asking two very simple questions:

• Are professionals spending a considerable amount of time on clerical duties, or are clerks forced into activities beyond their level of capability?

• Are there tasks that should be performed but are not being performed because of inadequate staffing?

If the answer to the second question is affirmative, as it frequently would be, it is likely that the tasks not being performed are professional ones. Clerical tasks tend to establish their own overriding priorities. Circulation returns must be shelved, cards must be filed, and books must be ordered, and all will take priority over online searches that have been requested. It is a rare (although brave) special librarian who consciously defers or neglects clerical duties to concentrate on professional ones in order to demonstrate or magnify the shortage of clerical support. It is a risky action precisely because many users of the special library, as well as nonusers in general administration and personnel departments, believe that clerical tasks *are* what a library does.

PROBLEMS OF CLERICAL STAFFING

Chapter 8 explained in some detail why it is a part of organizational strategy (often deliberately planned strategy) to minimize and curtail the levels of clerical staffing. This is particularly true for overhead organizations, for which there is frequently a lack of certainty about needed support levels, as well as a general perception that these levels are too great and should be reduced. Organizations that employ hiring freezes as the most "humane" (even if least organized) method for reducing staffing levels generally find that this results in a reduction and sometimes decimation of clerical staff.

The Impact of Attrition

A number of independent studies have shown turnover among clerks to be about three times as great as among professionals. As a consequence, when positions are eliminated through attrition, it is most frequently clerical positions that are lost. For many managers this strategy is acceptable, particularly in research or planning groups for which the gulf between professionals and clerks may be unbridgeable. During manpower curtailments the nucleus of the professional group remains; the group goes into semihibernation and waits for better times. During this period of waiting, at least the quality of staff—if not the quantity of output—is maintained, and the clear imbalance this action creates can sometimes serve to lift the clerical hiring freeze.

Special libraries and information centers usually do not have this luxury, because by and large they have not been successful in relating either the level of expectation or the level of actual performance to the resources provided. There is a real need to develop a clear relationship between service and resources, and between results and responsibility for decisions. One hopes that this change will come, but it will certainly only come gradually. In the interim, special librarians will continue to face the problems of how to perform clerical duties without adequate clerical staff.

There are no obvious answers to this problem, except the need to point out that where these circumstances exist, they should never be passively accepted as "reality." Management must be reminded how wasteful of organizational resources its policies are. All professionals must perform some clerical tasks, but when these tasks become repetitive or primary, something is wrong.

Alternatives to Clerical Staff

The application of computer technology provides considerable opportunities for replacing clerical tasks with computer-performed functions. This is likely to be an important option for the special library, in contrast to the average academic library, which has an ample pool of cheap student labor and also operates in an atmosphere that encourages such positions as a support for higher education. That value system is rare for special libraries and nonexistent for those in the for-profit sector.

The use of temporary or part-time personnel, the use of employees hired through agency agreements and the contracting out of entire functions sometimes provide alternatives in situations where money is more plentiful than people. It is preferable to contract clerical rather than professional duties. The work of contractors is easier to control in the performance of clerical tasks, and the professional duties provide greater prestige and visibility for the internal staff. In general, professional tasks should be contracted only when they require skills that are so esoteric as to be totally lacking internally, or when they demand only part-time or temporary application.

JOB CLASSIFICATIONS

None of these tactics for shifting clerical and professional duties works all of the time for most special libraries. Their managers are still left with the problem of differentiating between clerical and professional tasks.

Personnel Department Policies

Most organizational personnel departments understand the differentiation quite clearly, even if they don't see how it applies to special libraries. Stated most simply, the difference between clerks and professionals is the difference between employees paid hourly or weekly wages on the one hand and those paid monthly or annual salaries on the other.

On another level of comparison, it is the difference between job categories that are not exempt under the wage and hours laws from working overtime and so must be paid exactly for all hours worked, and those positions that are considered exempt under federal and state provisions. In general, exempt employees do not punch timeclocks or fill in time sheets. They are paid for what they accomplish rather than for how long it takes. Sometimes they end up working fewer hours, but more frequently they work extra time without extra pay. There are, of course, other benefits, which those librarians who have or aspire to professional status clearly recognize.

In general, special library managers would be wise to maintain the clear differentiation between clerks and professionals, which personnel departments understand very well, and not to undermine them with special requirements or special benefits. Clerks in most organizations operate at several levels of junior, intermediate and senior status, with salary scales to match. These general categories are perfectly adequate for the special library's needs.

Particular skills, such as the ability to type or file, or to meet and deal with the public, can emerge for certain jobs. However, these "special" attributes do not differ from those specified for other clerical jobs, which may require dexterity, endurance or the ability to drive a vehicle. It is when library managers try to develop specialized clerical job descriptions for individual clerks on a unique basis—such as senior clerical cataloging specialist—that they confuse personnel and wage and salary administrators. They also call into question the difference between these highly specific clerical duties and what professionals are supposed to do.

Paraprofessionals

The development of paraprofessionals, a group somewhere between clerks and professionals (often based on a two-year Associate of Arts degree or equivalent program), had a sharp upsurge during the 1960s but seems to have passed its peak. A clear and identified place seems to have been found for paramedical and paralegal employees. The library field, and in particular the special library field, does not have room for such esoteric distinctions. A special library with a staff of five or less (and such a category still encompasses the great majority of special libraries) would appear to lack room for five levels of specific job descriptions or three levels of employee benefits. In special libraries, paraprofessionals have in fact tended to be employed either in place of clerks or instead of professionals. The first usage is unfair to them and their additional training. The second is improper for both the organization and the library profession.

JOB DESCRIPTIONS AND EVALUATIONS

Special libraries, unlike academic and some public libraries, operate under personnel rules and procedures already established for the parent organization, which will not be modified to suit specialized requirements of the special library manager, whether these requirements are real or imaginary. Personnel policy and salary policy are usually based on the development of job descriptions, and then the evaluation of these descriptions into categories or levels for which salary ranges are established. This is considered important, because it provides a mechanism for a comparative evaluation of such disparate professional duties as accountant, economist, engineer, sales representative, chemist, production foreman and even librarian or technical information specialist, and thus for a salary balance which is fair and reasonable.

Wage and salary administrators have developed these tools over decades, and they will quite understandably resist the suggestion that our field requires something different. It is important that special librarians and information scientists recognize how jobs are ranked and evaluated. How they are paid is largely a function of this ranking, although questions of supply and demand also affect considerations. Supply and demand, however, is more likely to determine what salary within a range will be offered rather than which salary range applies.

The factors that count most heavily in the evaluation of positions include education, required experience, complexity of duties, supervisory responsibilities if any, amount of direct supervision received and impact of error. (This last simply means that if the incumbent makes a mistake, what problems can it cause?) It can be quickly noted that while each category is separately evaluated to provide a numerical total which then leads to a job level, there is room for some interchange.

Evaluating Experience

Most organizations that house special libraries, particularly in the for-profit sector, will not insist on specific educational qualifications but will permit an exchange of experience for education. Most frequently this is on the basis of "two years of experience equals one year of education." This is not unreasonable; the substitution of work experience for education is sometimes completely appropriate. However, it is necessary to define, for the purpose of job descriptions and for the benefit of personnel departments, what is meant by "experience." Experience does not simply mean longevity of employment; at least it should not and will not where union contract stipulations are not overriding. Experience means a period of planned and continued growth, with the assignment of greater responsibilities as earlier tasks are absorbed and mastered. It is not an automatic process, and it requires continued monitoring and evaluation.

Reasonable Requirements

While job descriptions cannot be allowed to deteriorate to meet the qualifications that are at hand, the reverse is also true. That is, they should not be unreasonably expanded beyond what is needed, simply to meet a qualification that an individual candidate happens to possess but that is not needed for the performance of the task. Such a strategy may work on one or two occasions, but it will inevitably result in a loss of the library manager's credibility. This will happen when you have to fill the position a second time and are forced to admit that the qualification stressed earlier, because the incumbent happened to possess it, is really not important after all.

Library managers should also be realistic in stating clerical qualifications. An ability to type can be a basic requirement. An ability to file can certainly be expected for a senior clerk. But familiarity with the Library of Congress classification scheme is undoubtedly an unreasonable expectation in a clerical job description. A manager may hope to acquire such skills without paying for them, but such an action also has the result of undermining the clear differentiation between professional and clerical work that personnel and salary analysts consider so important.

Not all clerks aspire to be promoted to professional duties (although they will probably accept professional salaries if they can get them). Not all clerks with such aspirations are capable of the required growth; those who are not must be told so. Finally, organizational needs for professionals are finite, and it has already been pointed out that in most cases the turnover of professionals is much slower than that of clerks. In other words, promotion also depends on opportunity as well as ability. This creates some inevitable limitations, because in successful organizations people are fitted to jobs that need to be done. Jobs are not created to meet the interests or preferences of individual employees, nor are they adapted to what people can do.

THE IMPACT OF UNIONS

Special library managers in organizations with unionized clerical staffs may find their options more curtailed, but only with regard to clerical hiring. They may be forced to accept the most senior qualified candidate, and they may be pressured to bend on the question of what "qualified" means. If qualifications are properly stated for clerical duties in the first place, however, they should be enforceable.

Union contracts never affect professional jobs, but negotiations may raise the question of which jobs are professional and which are clerical. Quite understandably, unions seek to broaden the definition of clerical positions to increase the jobs under their control. On occasion, personnel departments gladly cede some questionable positions into the union contract. They may find it is simpler to deal with such a position within the overall terms of the contract, or they may decide that monitoring the job description as a unique professional assignment may be more trouble than it is worth. When this occurs, or threatens to occur, for positions the special library or information center manager considers professional, it is clear evidence of a lack of communication and a lack of mutual understanding.

WORKING WITH PERSONNEL MANAGERS

It is not reasonable to expect personnel managers to understand library needs and priorities. By and large, they come from that group of professionals with little library experience as users, and most special libraries provide little support for the work of the personnel department. They would be well advised to begin to do so. Further, special librarians should attempt to understand the role and priorities of personnel managers and salary analysts.

Understanding Priorities

As already explained, the personnel department is a service organization which, like the library, makes no direct contribution to the efficiency of the organization. Like the library, its costs are easy to determine, but its contribution is more fugitive. Its priorities, like those of the special library, are directed to the support of those individuals and groups who are the wielders of power and makers of major decisions. Under the circumstances, it can be understood why wage and salary analysts have little patience for the review and revision of job descriptions for senior circulation clerks, catalog file maintenance assistants, bibliographic online search specialists and cataloging supervisors, when there is only one individual for each of these job descriptions.

Moreover, this author has never, in more than 20 years of special library management experience, found a wage analyst who understood why cataloging was a professional task, particularly when it is based or can be based on work already performed at the Library of Congress. They understand reference and bibliographic work as professional, and they may be cajoled or forced into approving professional job descriptions for others, but they remain unconvinced. The battle will resume anew every time job descriptions are changed or reviewed.

Simplifying the Wage and Salary Process

Special library managers should simplify the wage and salary process for themselves and by the same token for the personnel department. Most organizations have an adequate range of clerical job descriptions and salary ranges to suit even the most esoteric special library. Where specific skills are required—and they should clearly be required with caution to avoid blurring the delineation between these and professional duties—they can be accommodated within the evaluation ranges already mentioned. Most organizations that house special libraries, and particularly those in the for-profit sector, pay their clerks quite well, if and when they are willing to hire them. Sometimes they pay their clerks as well as their librarians.

As noted in Chapter 4, it is probably simpler to tie professional library job levels to those already developed for professional skills in heavy use within the organization. In a bank this plentiful job title may be economist. In other organizations it may be chemist, accountant or historian. Inevitably, two conditions exist. One is a system of job descriptions that can be built into a promotional ladder, through increased education, experience, complexity of duties or some combination of these factors. The second is that the salary structure for the most crucial skill the organization employs is invariably generous, usually more generous than the one in use for librarians and information specialists.

Adapting existing salary ranges and ladders already in place for the parent organization's key profession to librarians serves both the purposes of the information manager and those of the personnel administrator, who is now relieved of the onerous task—which is probably also perceived as unimportant—of trying to figure out what a descriptive cataloger is and does and how this person differs from a subject cataloger.

Square Pegs and Round Holes

One additional point must be made with regard to dealing with the personnel department. Personnel administrators operate under considerable pressures from operational managers, union representatives (in unionized organizations), and federal, state and local laws and guidelines. Their responsibility is not only to provide the best staff at the lowest cost, but to do so in a manner perceived to be fair and progressive, one that emphasizes promotions and minimizes terminations. With this background, it is easy to understand why personnel departments do a great deal of pounding square pegs into round holes. Sometimes this works, and it can be argued that the attempt is laudable in any case. However, it must be remembered that the function of the personnel department, like that of the legal department and of the security officer, has little direct relationship to how effectively other supervisors perform their own functions.

The personnel department head is not responsible for determining whether or not what is perceived as best from his or her point of view is in fact best or even acceptable for the library. That is the library manager's responsibility, and it is assumed in any organizationally dynamic environment that the library manager, like all other managers, will assure that his or her operation is not damaged in the process.

A certain amount of flexibility, under which candidates who are less than ideally suited but who are already internally available must be considered, is inevitable in any organization. In fact, it can be argued that it is the proper responsibility of any management to attempt to find new assignments for displaced employees whenever possible. For the library to accept its share of these placements is not necessarily unreasonable. It can be argued, however, that the special library as a very small unit does not have the luxury or flexibility for such treatment that larger units might enjoy. Unfortunately, the treatment of the special library is rarely one of balance or fairness. Instead, the library is frequently singled out as the assigned haven for those for whom no other appropriate assignment can be found.

The library as a personnel "dumping ground" is all too real a phenomenon for many special library administrators. Since it has already been postulated that there is no active conspiracy to harm the library, only two reasons for this emerge. The first, and clearly more important, is that personnel administrators do not recognize what a major difference their decision can make and what impact it might have on the overall effectiveness of the organization. An assignment to production management or marketing is perceived as having risk; an assignment to the special library is not. The second reason is that special librarians, frequently by the very nature of their humanist backgrounds and social concerns, can often be persuaded to share and accept these organizational misfits or displaced persons to a greater degree than other managers.

Solutions to this problem are neither easy nor pleasant. They depend first of all on establishing that what special libraries and information centers do is important and that it matters whether or not they do it well. Doing it well requires individuals with skill and vision, particularly because in a small staff lower levels of competence are not as easily absorbed. Ultimately, they depend also on a willingness to be assertive at all times, aggressive where appropriate, confrontational where necessary.

CONCLUSION

Chapter 8 stated that the responsibility of the special library is not the saving of money. It is also not the special librarian's responsibility to meet organizational personnel goals, whatever these may be. Others are well paid to monitor these activities. The special librarian's responsibility is that of managing an effective and useful special library or information center. Special library or information center managers must clearly spell out alternative approaches to problems, because in any dynamic organization there are alternatives. They must also specify what will happen if support is not provided.

Lack of support is a symptom of the greatest danger facing the special librarian. By and large libraries have no enemies, in part because they control no power base others covet, and in part because they still carry the residual perception that libraries are "good things." Rather, the greatest danger is that of being ignored, of not being taken seriously, of being patronized, of being trivialized.

SUGGESTED ADDITIONAL READINGS

Christianson, Elin B. *Paraprofessional and Nonprofessional Staff in Special Libraries*. New York: Special Libraries Association, 1973.

Green, Charlotte. "Nonprofessional Library Workers in the Science Libraries in Industry." *Special Libraries* 61:453-459 (October 1970).

Special Libraries: A Guide for Management, Second Edition. Op. cit.

13

Technology and the Special Library of the Future

Any attempt to forecast the status of special libraries and information centers is fraught with danger, since these institutions do not operate in an environment they can control. The frailty of the predictive process can easily be shown when we consider the impact of the oil embargo of the mid-1970s. This action, totally without warning from economists, arose from political considerations. However, it affected individual value systems, American consumer habits in the purchase of automobiles and home heating installations, and corporate decisions about whether to expand or to develop new product lines. The recession that followed had an impact on special libraries and information centers, an impact no writer in 1970 could possibly have predicted.

It was suggested in Chapter 2 that the successful development of special libraries and information centers in the United States and other nations with relatively uncontrolled economic systems was no coincidence. The impact of special libraries can only be felt in an environment in which rapid, accurate and cost-effective information makes a perceived difference and in which success carries reward. A totally controlled or egalitarian system is not a healthy environment for the development of professionally developed information mechanisms. This chapter assumes a continuation of some form of the capitalist profit system as a background for aggressive information services.

THE GROWTH OF INFORMATION

Given these assumptions, it is not difficult to reach several rather general conclusions. The rapid growth of information has been documented in many publications. Georges Anderla, in a 1974 study for the National Science Foundation, projected the growth of scientific publication alone at 8% per year, a figure which would lead to a doubling every nine years. If this rate of growth is accepted, the implications are particularly startling when we recognize that science and technology are not even any longer the fastest growing fields of publication as they were in the 1950s and 1960s.

Overwhelmed as we are with information sources contained in thousands of data bases and tens of thousands of journals, we are still forced to realize that this output is largely limited to the information productivity of only a handful of nations. We are just beginning to awaken to Japanese development and what it can teach us, and the contributions of the developing nations can only be conjectured.

In addition to the growth in the sheer bulk of information, we have also become aware of the increasing specialization and the growing interdependence of information. A scan of any comprehensive list of periodicals will quickly uncover subject fields of which the reader has never heard and confirm that there is a thriving literature in these fields. Moreover, the likelihood increases that the reader's own work will at some point put him into contact with at least the fringes of subject areas of which he may be only vaguely aware. Topics such as energy, environment, nutrition, pollution and education have become so multidimensional as to defy description and limitation.

THE INFORMATION ECONOMY AND THE SPECIAL LIBRARY

With growth and increasing complexity have come both an awareness of the importance of information for decision making and the realization that information should be accurate, complete, rapidly delivered and easily used. Unfortunately, this does not necessarily lead to a recognition of the importance of special libraries as the logical sources for this information. Some of the writers and speakers on the new and popular topic of "the information society" might be surprised to hear that they are talking about our area of responsibility and expertise. Such a claim would, in truth, be an exaggeration under present circumstances, in which many special libraries still concentrate on the acquisition, control and dissemination of documents, without much concern about their content. At the same time, this claim offers both opportunity and danger for special libraries.

Earlier chapters have stressed that the special library or information center may be ignored or starved but never hated. We have no enemies because we exercise little power and pose very little threat. Future developments could change this relationship. A striking example of the importance of the term "information" in the planning and decision process is that major and forward-looking industrial giants such as AT&T and IBM no longer refer to themselves as communications or computer companies. Instead, quite accurately, they refer to themselves as being in the information business.

Major studies about the development and impact of the information economy may never consider special libraries or information centers as a part of the spectrum. In fairness, special libraries have not been involved in the information economy, but this does not mean that they could not have been or could not be in the future. When a state government agency develops a job description for an information specialist who will gather and disseminate information on the factors affecting migrant labor, it describes a task closely resembling the work of a special librarian, but the agency does not know this. When a corporation establishes a task force to identify the international plant construction activities of its competitors and potential competitors, it is seeking information that competent special librarians with access to a range of data bases could have provided all along. The failure to realize that special librarians could do this is not new. What is new is the insistence that this be done at all.

The environment for special libraries will therefore undoubtedly change. The things we have wanted to do in the past but were not allowed to do will indeed be done, by us or by others. By the same token, the mundane and housekeeping tasks, which even our competitors are willing to leave to us, will not be worth doing at all, at least not in a professional setting.

THE IMPLICATIONS OF PRESENT TECHNOLOGY

In this environment, the impact of technology is not difficult to assess, because we are not considering future technology and the unforeseen changes it may bring. We are dealing with presently available and installed technology, about which there is virtually no uncertainty. Access to data bases is obtainable through terminals that can be located anywhere electrical power can be generated. As terminals and home computers become even more commonplace and less expensive, it is not difficult to predict that in 20—or perhaps even 10—years computers will be located in every home or office. Some universities are already beginning to require that students have computers in their dormitory rooms, much as engineering schools once required slide rules for their students.

ELECTRONIC ACCESS TO INFORMATION SOURCES

The general availability of computers, even if their primary use is for other business purposes or even for playing games, means that their owners will have direct access to bibliographic as well as other data bases on a worldwide basis. Whether they will want to exercise that capability or will prefer to continue to rely on an intermediary such as a special librarian is by no means certain. However, what does appear sure is that the capability for bypassing centralized library bibiliographic records will continue to expand, and at least some users are certain to take advantage of that opportunity. The monopoly that libraries historically exercised over some forms of bibliographic access will disappear; it is already beginning to wane.

The card catalog will probably be a curiosity in academic and special libraries by the turn of the century and may not even survive much longer in small public libraries. No tears should be shed for its demise and replacement by online catalogs, because its limitations have always caused tremendous restrictions for the entrepreneurial special librarian. Maintaining a card catalog requires a tremendous amount of time and energy, particularly from clerical staff, which as we already know, is usually a scarce resource in special libraries. Further, card catalogs are well suited for bibliographic descriptions that can be centered on the main entry card, but they are poor devices for subject retrieval, because card files do not permit coordinated term searching, at least not without considerable difficulty. Finally, and perhaps most subtly, the card catalog is, in the eye of the clientele, a link with past levels of service, which we are seeking to change.

Terminal access to bibliographic files provides unlimited entry to the holdings of the world at large. No longer will it really matter, except for proprietary documents, where an item is physically located. Ownership as a measure of quality will die hard in academic institutions, but it will die all the same. The growth of the literature, the increase in prices and the continuing pressures of budgets will make ownership unaffordable as it becomes increasingly irrelevant.

What will matter will not be what you own but what you can find and what you can deliver. Special librarians, forced by the paucity of their own holdings and by the breadth and time pressures of user demands into innovation and experimentation, are well ahead of their colleagues in the implementation of these ground rules and are far more ready psychologically to accept them.

INFORMATION DELIVERY

The transmittal of needed information will be through telephone lines and other electronic circuitry and via satellite. The technology exists at present, although it is expensive and still somewhat lacking in quality, particularly where multicolored medical diagrams are involved. However, if we know anything about technology, it is that it develops to meet needs. Processes will become cheaper, and quality will improve. We are already on the borders of a throw-away copy technology, in which copies of "borrowed" material are discarded after use rather than returned. Programs to disseminate government agency reports were already finding this process more economical than record keeping and return more than a decade ago.

Microstorage and transmittal with enlargement at the receiving end will certainly accelerate this process. It will mean the demise of circulation records, recall of material and overdue notices, except for very specialized and esoteric material, certainly not for routine books, reports and periodical articles. The process of "interlibrary loan" for periodical articles is already a complete misnomer. Articles are not lent; they are supplied and disposed of by the recipient. This change will free librarians from all of the grief that circulation records and overdue notices have historically caused in terms of client interactions and perceptions. It will also relieve much of the pressure of the clerical workload.

THE CONTINUING IMPORTANCE OF HARD COPY

The author does not share the view of F. Wilfrid Lancaster that ours will become a "paperless" society. Too many individuals like to have their own little proprietary hoard of article copies, SDI printouts and file reference cards. In addition, we know that computers are, among other things, rapid, inexpensive and increasingly high-quality *printing* devices. The major restriction for user files may be the parent organization's willingness to subsidize larger offices, book shelves and filing cabinets. These may well be looked at as fringe benefits, and if professionals consider them important to their well-being and prestige, they will retain them. Surely nobody believes that the size of offices has anything to do with the amount of space needed to perform one's work. It is a status symbol pure and simple. Individual personal literature collections may well achieve that status, particularly as that would differentiate the owner's office from the terminal-equipped one everyone else has. The amount of wall shelving and what is on it already constitute a significant status symbol in academia.

In the library itself, a basic collection of materials should be available for browsing and serendipitous access. Other materials—some books and certainly periodical articles and technical reports—will not be kept in full-sized printed form in the library, except perhaps for current issues. They will be retrieved from the electronic file on demand and presented to the user in the format which he or she prefers—display on a terminal, magnetic storage, microprint or full-sized copy. If it turns out after review that the material really was not needed after all, the error is hardly calamitous. The unwanted copy can simply be discarded.

COPYRIGHT AND DOWNLOADING

As noted in Chapter 11, copyright problems remain unresolved. The issues are complex, but solutions will be found because society adapts to attractive technological opportunities. Copying became absurdly simple with the invention of dry electrostatic copiers, and individuals began making copies. Copyright owners, who had little to fear while copying consisted of pencil and paper reproductions, quickly realized that they could not prevent copying. They could only seek to devise mechanisms for reimbursement when it occurs, and this remains the major concern of much of the present discussion.

Additional reimbursement mechanisms will undoubtedly be devised as copyright owners and data base producers come to grips with electronic file duplication, which goes far beyond the office copy machine in making the duplication of large amounts of information a very simple process. The copying of portions or all of files or individual records from a data base for internal use is called "downloading." It is already happening, although nobody can be quite sure to what extent. Negotiations for reimbursement have yet to take place except in individual cases, and this writer could not begin to speculate on the direction they will take, because they involve political pressures and alliances.

Regardless of the outcome, it will involve "only" money. Earlier chapters of this book have suggested that the operation of a library is a trivial cost to the parent organization. If the use of such downloaded file data is valuable, as it undoubtedly will, be then the costing mechanisms that are developed need not worry special librarians unduly, provided that costs can be predicted with reasonable accuracy and with enough advance warning to permit inclusion in the next budgetary process. Special library managers should concentrate on providing good services rather than saving money. They would be well advised to throw their influence behind mechanisms which permit the movement of information from one file to another, and leave to lawyers and cost accountants the negotiations of what represents a fair reimbursement.

LOCAL INFORMATION FILES

The preceding paragraphs have concentrated on the view that much information access will be global and not restricted by the physical facilities of the organization that houses the special library. This is not to suggest that local information files will disappear or become less important. Quite the contrary, unique and specialized files to fit the specific needs of the parent organization will grow in significance. They will come from two primary sources.

The first will continue to be local and sometimes proprietary files, unique to the interests of the organization and usually internally generated. As has already been stated, in many special library settings this body of information represents the potentially most important resource. At the same time, it is sometimes difficult to acquire. Authors, in full recognition of the axiom that knowledge is power, will sometimes attempt to withhold information from others in the same organization. Projects in direct competition are not unusual, and there is a particular aversion to the promulgation of negative information, the disclosure of tests that failed. The greatest opportunity for the special library in capturing such material quickly and completely is to acquire it for its own information files at the time of initial generation, which is now usually in computer form, thus avoiding the need to rekey it.

The second portion of internal files will come from the downloading of material of particular interest from larger and, frequently, commercially prepared files, for reuse and perhaps reformatting in the library.

MICROCOMPUTERS

The development of the microcomputer has opened a great many options for special librarians. Initially tied to large mainframe computers staffed by an organization-wide service that also provided systems and programming assistance, special libraries suffered from a lack of priority when this resource became scarce. The development of online search services with terminals tied to distant computer installations provided some flexibility of use, but relatively little cost or budget control. In a phenomenon which the information specialist and consultant Carlos Cuadra likens to that of the ticking taxi meter, special librarians were and still are apprehensive about mounting data base searches. In all too many cases, the sophistication of the available search strategy and the specialized knowledge of the searcher are both ignored in the attempt to get a "quick and dirty" answer and log off the system.

In addition, such centralized access services provide little support for internal functions of a clerical or routine nature and are not particularly practical for the housing of proprietary files. Although such arrangements do exist, they cause concerns about file security, as well as the fear of the ticking of that uncontrolled taxi meter. For many special and other libraries with controlled and finite budgets, the very open-ended nature of a search using a vendor-controlled data base causes serious problems. Many special libraries pass the cost of searching to user groups, an action that loses budgetary control and really provides the parent organization nothing except a more cosmetic display of cost allocations. As stated earlier, it is not an attractive alternative for the special library, which should budget and control all expenditures within its scope of responsibility. Clearly, this includes online searching.

Microcomputers have the potential to solve many of the special library's computer problems. As internally housed and uniquely dedicated equipment, they offer the special librarian far greater control over his or her work environment. They also provide much better control over the budgetary process, because the number of hours a microcomputer is used becomes irrelevant if you own it. (Of course, there are still telecommunications charges for searches of outside data bases.) In many cases the purchase of a microcomputer is made from separate organizational funds and does not affect the operating budget. Many software packages are commercially available, and it is reasonable to assume that the cooperation that has so characterized special librarianship will now extend to the sharing of experiences and internally developed programs for the same kind of equipment.

Finally, the use of microcomputers does not forfeit any of the options available on a mainframe system. Micros can be used as terminals to "talk to" major central computer installations and to transfer large tasks to the more appropriate installation. They can interact with microcomputers at other installations, including those of the same parent organization. Whether these special libraries are parts of a central system or separate institutions reporting to a local management becomes far less significant as bibliographic information is shared and requests for document delivery are transmitted. Microcomputers can also continue to serve as terminals for access to vendor-controlled data bases, to be searched directly or downloaded.

CONCLUSION

This chapter has not dealt heavily in either speculation or wishful thinking. The technology on which this look into the future is predicated exists today. It requires nothing more than qualitative refinement in some cases, cost reduction in others, and the development of both an understanding of potential use and the identification of needed software. There is ample evidence in the computer industry that where needs exist and rewards can be identified, those needs will be met.

What new technology lies around the corner? Specifics are impossible to predict. Without doubt, systems will exhibit greater flexibility, being either larger or smaller as needed. If smaller, they will also provide linkage to larger systems. They will be faster, they will be cheaper, and the output quality will be better. If progress continues only at a fraction of the pace exhibited in the last 25 years, it will still outstretch our imagination.

However, regardless of the technological specifics, the alternatives for special librarians seem clear enough. As clerical and housekeeping duties become increasingly routine and as access to information files continues to grow, the great need will be for individuals able and willing to analyze, interpret and repackage the bewildering array of information sources for application to specific problem solving. Writers like Daniel Bell have predicted that our society will witness an increased emphasis on activities other than manufacturing. The ten years since Bell's classic work certainly confirm that shift in emphasis and expenditure levels. In fact, some futurists now tell us that we are already past the post-industrial society and embarking on new, even more sophisticated courses.

For special librarians such discussions are not particularly important, because we can certainly see plenty of needed tasks that we are not performing. Others see them, too; they also see the prestige and power that these tasks bring. It is not at all certain that librarians will play a leading or major role in this developing scenario, although they certainly can and are probably best qualified to do it.

When information centers were first developed in the late 1950s and early 1960s, those proponents who came from outside our profession were careful to separate themselves from what librarians did. At the same time, they insisted that libraries were still necessary to supply the physical documents that were demanded as a result of their own activities. Some special librarians, fascinated by the promise of increased circulation statistics, were happy to embrace such a relationship. We now recognize it as a poor bargain that relegated these libraries to a permanently perceived clerical status.

In any case, that bargain is no longer available to us. New delivery mechanisms will make library clerical activities, such as lending and recall, automatic or even eliminate them altogether. Either we will mature fully as information specialists and information intermediaries, or we may disappear entirely.

SUGGESTED ADDITIONAL READINGS

Bell, Daniel. *The Coming of Post-Industrial Society; A Venture in Social Forecasting*. New York: Basic Books, Inc., 1973.

Lancaster, F. Wilfrid. *Toward Paperless Information Systems*. New York: Academic Press, Inc. 1978.

Porat, Marc Uri. *The Information Economy*. Ann Arbor, MI: University Microfilms International, 1979.

Selected Bibliography

Adams, Scott. "The National Library of Medicine." Chapter 11 in *The Handbook of Medical Library Practice*, Third Edition, edited by Gertrude L. Annan and Jacqueline W. Felter. Chicago: Medical Library Association, 1970, pp. 331-346.

Bailey, Martha J. "Functions of Selected Company Libraries/Information Services." *Special Libraries* 72:18-30 (January 1981).

— — —. "Middle Managers Who Are Heads of Company Libraries/Information Services." *Special Libraries* 70:507-518 (December 1979).

Bauer, Charles K. "Managing Management." *Special Libraries* 71:204-216 (April 1980).

Becker, Joseph. "How to Integrate and Manage New Technology in the Library." *Special Libraries* 74:1-6 (January 1983).

Bell, Daniel. *The Coming of Post-Industrial Society: A Venture in Social Forecasting*. New York: Basic Books, Inc., 1973.

Birchette, Kathleen P. "The History of Medical Libraries from 2000 B.C. to 1900 A.D." *Bulletin of the Medical Library Association* 61:302-308 (July 1973).

Boaz, Martha. "Evaluation of Special Library Service for Upper Management." *Special Libraries* 59: 789-791 (December 1968).

Boss, Richard W. "The Library as an Information Broker." *College & Research Libraries* 40:136-140 (March 1979).

— — —. *The Library Manager's Guide to Automation, 2nd Edition*. White Plains, NY: Knowledge Industry Publications, Inc., 1984.

Brodman, Estelle. "The Delivery of Medical Information in the 1970s." *Bulletin of the Medical Library Association* 59:579-584 (October 1971).

Christianson, Elin B. *Paraprofessional and Nonprofessional Staff in Special Libraries*. New York: Special Libraries Association, 1973.

— — —. "Special Libraries: Putting Knowledge to Work." *Library Trends* 25:399-416 (July 1976).

— — — and Janet L. Ahrensfeld. "Toward a Better Understanding of New Special Libraries." *Special Libraries* 71:146-153 (March 1980).

Cowgill, Logan O. and Robert J. Havlik. "Standards for Special Libraries." *Library Trends* 21:249-260 (October 1972).

Curtis, John and Stephen Abram. "Special and Corporate Libraries: Planning for Survival and Success." *Canadian Library Journal* 40:225-228 (August 1983).

Dagnese, Joseph M. "Cooperation between Academic and Special Libraries." *Special Libraries* 64:423-432 (October 1973).

DeGennaro, Richard. "Library Automation: Changing Patterns and New Directions" *Library Journal* 101:175-183 (January 1, 1976).

Dodd, James B. "The Gap in Standards for Special Libraries." *Library Trends* 31:85-91 (Summer 1982).

— — —. "Information Brokers." *Special Libraries* 67:243-250 (May/June 1976).

Drake, Miriam A. "The Management of Libraries as Professional Organizations." *Special Libraries* 68:181-186 (May/June 1977).

Drucker, Peter F. "Managing the Public Service Institution." *College & Research Libraries* 37:4-14 (January 1976).

Echelman, Shirley. "Libraries Are Businesses Too!" *Special Libraries* 65:409-414 (October/November 1974).

Epstein, H. "Technology of Libraries and Information Networks." *Journal of the American Society for Information Science* 31:425-437 (November 1980).

Ferguson, Elizabeth. "The What, Why, How of Annual Reports." *Special Libraries* 47:203-206 (June 1956).

Garvey, William D. *Communication, The Essence of Science.* Elmsford, NY: Pergamon Press, Inc., 1979.

Garvin, David. "The Information Analysis Center and the Library." *Special Libraries* 62:17-23 (January 1971).

Green, Charlotte. "Nonprofessional Library Workers in the Science Libraries in Industry." *Special Libraries* 61:453-459 (October 1970).

Grosch, Audrey N. *Minicomputers in Libraries, 1981-82: The Era of Distributed Systems.* White Plains, NY: Knowledge Industry Publications, Inc., 1982.

Hamilton, Beth A. "Principles, Programs and Problems of a Metropolitan Multitype Library Cooperative." *Special Libraries* 67:19, 23-29 (January 1976).

Hedberg, Bo, et al. "Camping on Seesaws: Prescriptions for a Self-Designing Organization." *Administrative Science Quarterly* 21(1):41-65 (March 1976).

Hendricks, Donald B. "The Regional Medical Library Program." *Library Trends* 24:331-345 (October 1975).

Hull, David and Henry D. Feamley. "The Museum Library in the United States: A Sample." *Special Libraries* 67:289-298 (July 1976).

Jackson, Eugene B. and Ruth L. Jackson. "Characterizing the Industrial Special Library Universe." *Journal of the American Society for Information Science* 31:208-214 (May 1980).

Jonker, Frederick. "The Termatrex Inverted 'Punched Card' System." *American Documentation* 11:305-315 (October 1960).

Kaegbein, Paul and Renate Sindermann. "Cooperation among Special Libraries at the International Level." *Special Libraries* 72:390-398 (October 1981).

Kaske, Neal K. and Nancy Sanders. "Networking and the Electronic Library." *Library Quarterly* 17:65-76 (Fall 1981).

Kates, Jacqueline R. "One Measure of a Library's Contribution." *Special Libraries* 65:332-336 (August 1974).

Kilgour, Frederick G. "Computer-Based Systems, a New Dimension to Library Cooperation." *College & Research Libraries* 34:137-143 (March 1973).

Kingman, Nancy M. and Carol Vantine. "The Special Librarian/Fee-Based Service Interface." *Special Libraries* 68:320-322 (September 1977).

Kok, John. "Now That I'm in Charge, What Do I Do?" *Special Libraries* 71:523-528 (December 1980).

Kruzas, Anthony T. *Business and Industrial Libraries in the United States.* New York: Special Libraries Association, 1965.

Lancaster, F. Wilfrid. *Toward Paperless Information Systems.* New York: Academic Press, Inc., 1978.

Landau, Herbert B. "Contract Services in the Special Library: The Make or Buy Decision." *Special Libraries* 64:175-180 (April 1973).

Lechner, Marian G. "Organization of a Recreational Library." In *Readings in Special Librarianship*, edited by Harold S. Sharp. New York: Scarecrow Press, Inc., 1963, pp. 114-121.

"Library Committees—Pro and Con." *Special Libraries* 50:235-243 (July/August 1959).

Luhn, Hans Peter. "Keyword-in-Context Index for Technical Literature." *American Documentation* 11:288-295 (October 1960).

Mason, Marilyn Gell. *The Federal Role in Library and Information Services.* White Plains, NY: Knowledge Industry Publications, Inc., 1983.

Matarazzo, James M. *Closing the Corporate Library: Case Studies on the Decision Making Process*. New York: Special Libraries Association, 1981.

— — —. "Lessons from the Past: Special Libraries in Times of Retrenchment." *Canadian Library Journal* 40:221-223 (August 1983).

Murphy, Marcy. "Networking Practices and Priorities of Special and Academic Librarians: A Comparison." University of Illinois Graduate School of Library Science Occasional Paper No. 126, December 1976.

Newman, Wilda B. "Managing a Report Collection for Zero Growth." *Special Libraries* 71:276-282 (May/June 1980).

Park, Margaret K. "Computer-Based Bibliographic Retrieval Services: The View from the Center." *Special Libraries* 64:187-192 (April 1973).

— — —. "Decision-Making Processes for Information Managers." *Special Libraries* 72:307-318 (October 1981).

Phyrr, Peter A. "Zero Base Budgeting." *Harvard Business Review* 48:111-121 (November/December 1970).

Pings, Vern M. "Regional Medical Libraries: A Concept and a Necessity." *Bulletin of the Medical Library Association* 59:242-246 (April 1971).

Pizer, Irwin. "Biomedical Libraries." *Special Libraries* 69:296-299 (August 1978).

Porat, Marc Uri. *The Information Economy*. Ann Arbor, MI: University Microfilms International, 1979.

Pratt, Allan D. "Use of Microcomputers in Libraries." *Journal of Library Automation* 13:7-17 (March 1980).

Randall, Gordon E. "Budgeting for a Company Library." *Special Libraries* 58:166-172 (March 1967).

Robertson, W. Davenport. "A User-Oriented Approach to Setting Priorities for Library Service." *Special Libraries* 71:345-353 (August 1980).

Robinson, Barbara M. "The Role of Special Libraries in the Emerging National Network." *Special Libraries* 72:8-17 (January 1981).

Russell, Dolores E. "Records Management: An Introduction." *Special Libraries* 65:17-21 (January 1974).

Sass, Samuel. "Must Special Libraries Be Parasites?" *Special Libraries* 50:149-154 (April 1959).

Severson-Tris, Mary A. "The Map Library in Private Industry." *Special Libraries* 69:94-99 (March 1978).

Shaughnessy, Thomas W. "Technology and the Structure of Libraries." *Libri* 32:149-155 (June 1982).

Special Libraries: A Guide for Management, Second Edition. New York: Special Libraries Association, 1981.

Special Libraries Association. "Information Technology and Special Libraries." *Special Libraries* 72: entire issue (April 1981).

— — —. "Objectives and Standards for Special Libraries." *Special Libraries* 55:672-680 (December 1964). Also issued as *Objectives for Special Libraries*. New York: Special Libraries Association, 1970.

— — —. *SLA Triennial Salary Survey*. New York: Special Libraries Association, 1983. (Planned for repetition every three years.)

Steuerman, Clara. "Music Libraries." *Special Libraries* 69:425-428 (November 1978).

Stinson, E. Ray. "Standards for Health Sciences Libraries." *Library Trends* 31:125-137 (Summer 1982).

Taube, Mortimer. *Computers and Common Sense: The Myth of Thinking Machines*. New York: Columbia University Press, 1961.

Trueswell, Richard W. "Some Behavioral Patterns of Library Users: The 80/20 Rule." *Wilson Library Bulletin* 44:458-461 (January 1969).

Tudor, Dean. "The Special Library Budget." *Special Libraries* 63:517-527 (November 1972).

Waldron, Helen J. "The Business of Running a Special Library." *Special Libraries* 62:63-70 (February 1971).

Walker, William B. "Art Libraries: International and Interdisciplinary." *Special Libraries* 69:476-481 (December 1978).

White, Herbert S. "An American Federation of Library Associations: The Time Has Come." *Library Journal* 107:860-864 (May 1, 1982).

— — —. "Cost-Effective and Cost-Benefit Determinations in Special Libraries." *Special Libraries* 70:163-169 (April 1979).

— — —. "Growing User Information Dependence and Its Impact on the Library Field." *ASLIB Proceedings* 31(2):74-87 (February 1979).

— — —. "Management: A Strategy for Change." *Canadian Library Journal* 35:329-339 (October 1978).

— — —. "Mechanized Information Processing and the Librarian." *Canadian Library* 19:64-69 (September 1962).

— — —. "Organizational Placement of the Special Library, Its Relationship to Success and Survival." *Special Libraries* 64:141-144 (March 1973).

— — —. "Toward Professionalism." *Special Libraries* 60:69-73 (February 1969).

Williams, Martha E. "Criteria for Evaluation and Selection of Data Bases and Data Base Services." *Special Libraries* 66:561-569 (December 1975).

Index

ABOUT THE AUTHOR

Herbert S. White is dean of the School of Library and Information Science, Indiana University. He was previously senior vice president, Institute for Scientific Information; executive director, NASA Scientific and Technical Information Facility; and program manager, IBM Corporate Technical Information Center.

White is former president of both the Special Libraries Association and the American Society for Information Science; treasurer and member of the executive committee, International Federation for Documentation; director, American Federation of Information Processing Societies; chairman, Governmental Relations Committee, Association of American Library Schools; and member, American Library Association Committee on Accreditation.

Widely known as a writer, speaker and consultant, he is the author of *Publishers and Libraries—A Study of Scholarly and Research Journals* (with Bernard M. Fry, 1976) and more than 50 articles and book chapters. He won the 1976 ASIS award for Information Science Book of the Year and has won numerous other awards for research papers.

White holds a B.S. in chemistry from the College of the City of New York and an M.L.S. from Syracuse University.